"Nolo's home page is worth bookmark[ing]"
—WALL STREET JOURNAL

W9-AUW-068

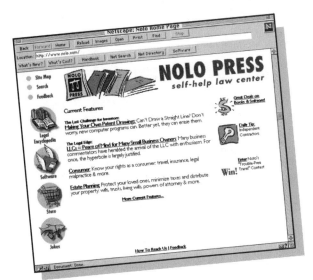

LEGAL INFORMATION ONLINE

www.nolo.com

24 hours a day

AT THE NOLO PRESS SELF-HELP LAW CENTER ON THE WEB, YOU'LL FIND

- Nolo's comprehensive Legal Encyclopedia, with links to other online resources
- Downloadable demos of Nolo software and sample chapters of many Nolo books
- An online law store with a secure online ordering system
- Our ever-popular lawyer jokes
- Discounts and other good deals, our hilarious Shark Talk game

THE NOLO NEWS

Stay on top of important legal changes with Nolo's quarterly magazine, *The Nolo News*. Start your free one-year subscription by filling out and mailing the response card in the back of this book. With each issue, you'll get legal news about topics that affect you every day, reviews of legal books by other publishers, the latest Nolo catalog, scintillating advice from Auntie Nolo and a fresh batch of our famous lawyer jokes.

Second Edition

QUICK & LEGAL

WILL
BOOK

by Attorney Denis Clifford

NOLO PRESS BERKELEY

YOUR RESPONSIBILITY WHEN USING A SELF-HELP LAW BOOK

We've done our best to give you useful and accurate information in this book. But laws and procedures change frequently and are subject to differing interpretations. If you want legal advice backed by a guarantee, see a lawyer. If you use this book, it's your responsibility to make sure that the facts and general advice contained in it are applicable to your situation.

KEEPING UP TO DATE

To keep its books up to date, Nolo Press issues new printings and new editions periodically. New printings reflect minor legal changes and technical corrections. New editions contain major legal changes, major text additions or major reorganizations. To find out if a later printing or edition of any Nolo book is available, call Nolo Press at 510-549-1976 or check the catalog in the *Nolo News,* our quarterly newspaper or contact us on the Internet at www.nolo.com.

To stay current, follow the "Update" service in the *Nolo News.* You can get a free one-year subscription by sending us the registration card in the back of the book. In another effort to help you use Nolo's latest materials, we offer a 25% discount off the purchase of the new edition your Nolo book when you turn in the cover of an earlier edition. (See the "Special Upgrade Offer" in the back of the book.) This book was last revised in January 1999.

SECOND EDITION	January 1999
PRODUCTION	Stephanie Harolde
EDITORS	Lisa Goldoftas & Stephen Elias
PROOFREADER	Robert Wells
INDEX	Jane Meyerhofer
BOOK DESIGN	Nancy Erb
PRINTING	Delta Lithograph
COVER DESIGN	Toni Ihara

Clifford, Denis
    The quick and legal will book / by Denis Clifford. — 2nd ed.
        p.   cm.
    Includes index.
    ISBN 0-87337-505-X
    1. Wills—United States—Popular works. 2. Wills—United States–
–Forms. I. Title.
KF755.Z9C55 1999
346.7305' 4—dc21   98-39722
                                CIP

Dedication

To my mother, Katherine Corbett Clifford. As her brother said when they were young, "Not like the other girls."

Acknowledgements

Once again, writing a Nolo book was a group effort and could not have been done without the contributions of many of my colleagues here. Specifically, Lisa Goldoftas, a wonderful, thorough editor and lively spirit; Steve Elias, the soul of Nolo, old friend and brilliant editor; Stephanie Harolde, unique and irreplaceable production assistant, editor, writer, friend; Mike Edwards and Ling Yu, of Nolo Press Customer Service, who gave time generously to read and review the manuscript; Nancy Erb for her wizard-work with computers, doing the layout for the book. Finally, I want to thank all my fellow Noloids. Each one truly contributes to making this enterprise both productive and such an enjoyable place to work, or party.

CONTENTS

CHAPTER 1

HOW THIS BOOK WORKS

CHAPTER 2

YOUR BENEFICIARIES

APPENDIX

How This Book Works

This book is for people who want to make a basic will—nothing complex, no frills, just a valid will that does the job. It is for people who want to leave their property outright (no strings attached) when they die. The key to doing this is simplicity.

If you've bought this book, you probably know that a will is a legal document where you specify which people and organizations will receive which of your property after you die. You may also use a will to name an adult to be responsible for your minor children's personal care and finances.

Following the step-by-step instructions in this book, you can create your own basic will that:

- leaves your property to the people and organizations you choose
- names someone to care for your minor children
- names someone to manage property you leave to minor children, including your own children, and
- names your executor, the person with authority to make sure that the terms of your will are carried out.

ICONS USED IN THIS BOOK

To aid you in using the book, I use four icons.

 CAUTION ICON: A caution about potential problems.

 FAST TRACK ICON: "Fast track" lets you know that you may be able to skip some material.

 RESOURCE ICON: Refers you to another self-help resource.

 LAWYER ICON: Situations when I recommend that you see a lawyer about a particular issue.

A. Who Can Use a Basic Will?

By and large, people who need only a basic will are under age 50 and own property worth less than the threshold limit for federal estate taxes ($650,000 in 1999, rising to $1 million in 2006). As one grows older, a basic will may not be the most economical and efficient method for passing your property. Certain types of more sophisticated planning may be desirable, which generally aren't called for with younger people. (See Section B, below, for more on this topic.)

This book contains five sample will forms that are valid in every state and Washington, D.C., with the exception of Louisiana (which has unique laws governing wills). These will forms have been carefully prepared to keep your work to a quite manageable amount.

WILL WRITING TERMS DEFINED

In discussing wills, I've tried to reduce legal jargon to a minimum. There are a few words or concepts you'll need to understand (but probably many fewer than you feared).

Beneficiaries or primary beneficiaries. These are the people or institutions you choose to leave some or all of your property to. People preparing a basic will usually are clear on who their beneficiaries are: a spouse or mate, children and perhaps a few friends or charities.

Alternate Beneficiaries. These are the people or institutions you name to receive your property if your primarily beneficiary dies before you.

Property. Everything you own. This can range from real estate ("real property," in legalese) to stocks, jewelry, cars, collectibles, clothes and every other item you own.

Gifts. Throughout this book, the word "gift" or "gifts" is used to refer to property you leave by your will. Sometimes lawyers distinguish between "devises," which are gifts of real estate, and "bequests," which are gifts of any other kind of property. I'm happy to avoid this legalese by the use of the direct, and accurate, word "gift." In a different context, the word "gift" can also be used to refer to property freely transferred while all involved are living—from a small holiday gift to a substantial gift of cash.

Executor. This is the person you name to have authority to carry out the terms of your will. In some states, this person is also called your "personal representative" or "administrator."

Estate Planning. This term covers several different concerns. First is arranging for the transfer of your property, after your death, in the most economical and efficient manner. Such planning requires time and, quite often, money. Other aspects of estate planning include providing for minor children (see Chapter 4, Children), saving on death taxes and arranging for the handling of your personal and financial affairs if you become incapacitated. (See Chapter 6, Estate Planning.)

B. About Probate and Taxes

You've probably heard of probate and know it has a dubious reputation (well earned). In probate, the will of a person who died is filed with a court, property is located and gathered by an estate executor. Debts and taxes still owed are paid and the remaining property is distributed as the will directs. Most property passed by will must go through probate.

Probate certainly has drawbacks. It can be lengthy, commonly taking a year or more. And it can also be expensive, normally requiring the services of lawyers and perhaps other specialists. However fees for these experts are determined (they vary by state), payment will always come out of property you intended for family and friends.

The good news is that people whose situations warrant a basic will have little reason to concern themselves now with probate. People using basic wills are usually relatively young. Their real concern is to make legal arrangements for the statistically unlikely event that they die suddenly and unexpectedly. Yes, with a will there is a risk that their property may end up in probate, but accepting that risk is, for most younger people, preferable to creating complex and often costly estate plans many years before they're likely to come into play. (See Chapter 6, Estate Planning, Sections A and B, for more about probate and common ways to avoid it.)

Similarly, because most young people don't have large amounts of property, they can usually safely wait to consider whether they need to make plans to save on federal estate taxes.

If your net worth is $650,000 or more: Your estate consists of the net worth of all the property you own when you die, in whatever form of ownership. Net worth is the market value of the property, less any amounts owed on it. While all estates are (theoretically) subject to federal estate taxes, the *personal estate tax exemption* allows a set dollar amount of property to be transferred free of tax. For 1999, the exempt amount is $650,000; this amount will rise to $1 million for 2006 and thereafter. I use the term *estate tax threshold* to mean the range of exempt amounts, from $650,000 to $1 million.

People with estates above the estate tax threshold should consider estate planning beyond the scope of this book. If your property, whether individually or combined as a couple exceeds the estate tax threshold, you may be able to save large amounts of money from the tax man by using more sophisticated planning methods than preparing a basic will. The rudiments of estate tax planning are discussed in Chapter 6, Section C.

C. Can You Safely Use This Book?

Let me reassure you at the start that preparing a basic will is not hard for most people. Some lawyers routinely use scare tactics designed to frighten people into believing that preparing a will is such a complex, technical process that no non-lawyer dare risk it. This is nonsense. Pause for a moment and consider what a basic will actually is and does. In essence, a basic will is an instrument to transfer your own property to whomever you want to get it. What's hard about that? Indeed, in most societies, including other Western cultures, the will-writing and transfer process is routine, without the necessity for lawyers or courts.

This book, and the will forms it contains, will enable most readers to prepare a basic will without having to pay for a lawyer. The heart of the will-making process consists of deciding who gets what, thus the most complicated decision you'll make is who you want to receive your property. If your desires are clear and uncomplicated, you can make your own will.

Take a common situation, where both members of a married couple want to leave their property to the other spouse. If that spouse isn't alive, then all property is to be divided equally between their kids. What the couple wants can be said in two sentences. Why should transferring their simple desire in a valid legal document be so difficult that an expert must be paid? This book is based on the truth that there's no reason to involve a costly expert if a will writer's desires are direct and uncomplicated.

Now let's look at a few real life situations where a basic will from this book will work fine.

Example 1: *Nyrit and Jerome, in their 30s, own a home (although, except for paying for repairs, it sure can seem that the bank owns it), two cars and some savings. Their net estate totals $90,000. They have one child, Mark, age 12. Each prepares a will leaving all his or her property to the other. If they die together, Mark is to receive all their property. Nyrit and Jerome agree that Nyrit's brother Iraz will care for Mark and manage the property until Mark turns 18.*

Example 2: *Sam, a widower, owns property with a net worth of $260,000. He has three adult children. He creates a will leaving all his property equally to his children. He specifies that if any child dies before him, that child's share is to be divided equally between the surviving children.*

Example 3: *Barbara is a single mother with two teenaged children. Though she's not on amicable terms with her ex-husband, she does admit he tries to be a decent father ("within his self-absorbed limits") and does pay child support payments more or less on time. Barbara prepares a will leaving all her property equally to her children. Because Barbara does not want her husband managing money left to her children if she dies, she uses her will to appoint her sister Debbie to manage each child's property until that child turns 18.*

PEOPLE WHO SHOULD NOT USE THIS BOOK

If you have any complexities in your family situation, your property or your beneficiary plans, this book is not for you. I could go on for pages trying to define what "complexities" are, but I believe I can rely on readers' common sense here. I'll offer a few specific examples of situations where you'd need to consult a lawyer to safely prepare your will:

- You want to create a trust protecting property for two generations—for example, you want to leave some property in trust for your child, with that property to go to that child's children (your grandchildren) when your child dies.
- A child or family member has a disability or other special needs that you wish to address in your will when leaving that person property.
- You are in a second or subsequent marriage where there are children from a prior marriage and you believe there is a real potential for conflict—the desires and expectations of children from a former marriage versus those of the current spouse, and whatever other children may be involved. By contrast, there are certainly many second/subsequent marriages where such conflicts are unlikely. In that case, you can safely use a will from this book if it fits your other needs.
- You believe that someone might contest your will. The grounds for contesting a will are that the will writer was not mentally competent when writing it, or the will was procured by fraud or duress (such as some evil doer exerting undue influence over the will writer). I do want to assure you that will contests are quite rare and it's even more rare that anyone succeeds in overturning a will. Happily, the great majority of people don't face any realistic possibility of someone contesting their will.

Finally, in Chapter 11, Going Further, I discuss a number of concerns not covered in this book that can be addressed by other Nolo self-help resources.

D. Real Life

Preparing a will may seem minor in the face of the intense emotional force and mystery of death. Although this is not a philosophical or spiritual book, I do want to note that the emotional realities involved in a death are profound. But however one chooses to deal with death spiritually or philosophically, there are practical issues that must be confronted. A will is the easiest way to handle most of these important practical matters.

It's also important to acknowledge that the process of writing a will is more than a practical necessity. Deciding who you want to receive your property after your death can be a significant process. The peace of mind one achieves by preparing a will—having all that nagging list of "really should be dones" behind you—is very real and satisfying. Certainly it's no denigration of death, or life, for you to be concerned with the wisest and most desirable distribution of your property.

In spite of this, the unfortunate reality is that many Americans still don't have a will. Why not? No one knows for sure, but here are my hunches:

- *Lack of reliable information.* The legal establishment has managed to mystify the process of writing a will. People are fearful of making mistakes by doing it themselves or don't know they can prepare their own will. In fact, no law requires that a will be drafted or approved by a lawyer.

- *Cost.* People understandably resist paying a hunk of money to a lawyer for what their intuition tells them shouldn't be a difficult or complicated task.

- *Superstition.* Some people fear that just thinking about the practical consequences of one's death could somehow hasten death's arrival. We know better, right?

- *Good old procrastination.* For anyone with loved ones, it's certainly a bad idea to risk dying without a will, which leaves the distribution of one's estate for state law to determine. (This is called "dying intestate.")

WHAT HAPPENS IF YOU DIE WITHOUT A WILL?

Since you've bought this book and intend to make a will, I won't badger you with dire warnings about what would happen if you die without a will. (Anyway, I never did manage to be an effective badgerer.) To put it simply—if you die without a valid will (or other valid property transfer device), your state law specifies who gets your property. That property is always divided among close family members, as the law requires. No flexibility is allowed. Perhaps worse, the person supervising the distribution of your property (and receiving a fee for services) will be someone appointed by a probate judge, not anyone you've chosen. If you have minor children and the other parent isn't involved, a court would appoint a guardian for your children without your input. And certainly there have been instances where such a person was far more concerned with extracting hefty fees from your property than with your children's well-being. Enough said?

E. Considerations for Parents of Minor Children

Being a parent of young children may have motivated you to buckle down to the task of writing your will in the first place. Although contemplating the possibility of your early death can be wrenching, it is important to adopt the best contingency plan for the care of your children. If the other parent is available and willing, he or she can handle the task. But life is full of possibilities, some of them rather bleak. You and the other parent might die close together in time. Or, you may be a single parent who needs to come to terms with what would happen if you die while your children are young and the other parent is unable or unwilling to assume responsibility.

Finally, some parents don't want the other parent to gain custody, because they believe that he or she isn't sufficiently responsible or loving. Chapter 4, Children, Section A, addresses this concern. I summarize it here by stating that there isn't much you can do to prevent the other parent gaining custody, unless that parent can be proved to be legally unfit to raise the children.

When planning for the possibility of your early death, you'll need to answer two important questions

- *Who do you want to care for your minor children?* Perhaps the most crucial decision is who will raise your child(ren) if you and the other parent cannot. This is an extremely personal matter. I've found that most people know, by the time they begin to prepare a will, who they want to choose—and they've discussed this possible responsibility with the person of their choice, who has agreed to accept it.

- *Who can manage property you (or others) leave your children?* If your minor children may inherit valuable property from you, that property will have to be managed by a responsible adult. Except for items of little value, minors are not permitted by law to assume legal control over property left to them in a will. It is vitally important to your children's interests that you arrange for this management yourself, in your will, rather than leave it up to a court to appoint and supervise a property manager.

Chapter 4, Children, assists you through the decision-making processes regarding custody and care of, and property management for, your minor children.

F. Legal Overview

There are surprisingly few legal restrictions and requirements in the will-making process. Let's look at the basic rules.

1. Who Can Make a Will?

If you're an adult, you can create a legally valid will as long as you meet the following two criteria:

You must be at least 18 years of age (19 years of age if you live in Wyoming). Some states allow younger people to make a will if they are married, in the military or are legally emancipated (have achieved adult status by order of a court).

You must be "of sound mind." This means you must:

- know what a will is, what it does and that you are making one
- understand the relationship between yourself and those you would normally provide for in your will, such as a spouse or children, and
- understand the kind and quantity of property you own and how to distribute it.

In real world terms, a person must be pretty far gone before his or her will could be invalidated by a judge on grounds of the will writer's incompetence. For instance, forgetfulness, or some diminution of memory capacity, isn't sufficient. If you can read and understand this book, your mind is plenty sound enough to prepare a valid will.

2. Will Requirements

The laws in each state control whether a will made by a resident of that state is valid. You should make your will in the state where you live. If you move to another state, don't worry. A will that is valid in the state where it was made is also valid in all other states.

If you're temporarily living outside the United States, your state is where you have your permanent residence (or "state of record," if in the military). If you are living outside the United States permanently, do not use this book.

Following are the bare bones legal requirements to make a valid will. The will must:

- include at least one substantive provision—either giving away some property or naming a guardian to care for minor children who are left without parents

- be signed and dated by the person making it, and

- be witnessed by two people (three in Vermont) who are not named as beneficiaries under the will.

Also strongly advisable is that the will:

- name someone with authority to enforce the terms of the will (your executor), and

- be comprehensible. No nonsensical, legalistic-sounding language, such as "I hereby give, bequeath and devise," is necessary.

Contrary to what many people believe, a will need not be notarized to be legally valid.

3. Handwritten Wills

Unwitnessed, handwritten wills—in legalese, "holographic wills"—are legally valid only in some states, not the majority. And handwritten wills are risky, even where legal. Most obviously, after your death, it may be difficult to prove that an unwitnessed, handwritten document was actually written by you and that you intended it to be your will. Further, many judges are hostile to handwritten wills, which are often held to very strict standards.

A word processed or typed, properly signed and witnessed will is much less vulnerable than a handwritten one to challenge by anyone claiming it was forged or fabricated. If need be, witnesses can later testify in court that the person whose name is on the will is the same person who signed it, and that making the will was a voluntary and knowing act. Also, there is a simple legal document called a self-proving affidavit that, if signed by the will writer and the witnesses before a notary, will make it easier to get the will accepted in court. (See Chapter 8, Preparing Your Final Will, Section D.)

4. Other Types of Wills

A few states accept the historical leftover of oral (spoken) wills, but only under very limited circumstances, such as when a mortally wounded soldier utters last wishes. Oral wills, even in the states that accept them, are of no use for people in normal life situations who don't fit into the narrow categories permitted.

Finally, you may have heard of audiovisual wills, in which you are filmed (videotaped) as you speak your will desires. Audiovisual wills are not legally valid wills, because no state legislature has authorized them.

G. How to Proceed

This book is designed to lead you, sequentially, through the steps you'll need to take to prepare your own will. Chapters 2 through 5 discuss the heart of making a will: who gets what, what will happen to your children, who will you name to be your executor. Finally, Chapter 6 gives a brief look at going beyond a basic will into general estate planning.

Chapter 7 contains detailed step-by-step instructions for completing each of the five sample will forms contained in the Appendix. Depending on your marital status and whether or not you have children, you'll select the will form appropriate for you and carefully prepare a rough draft.

In Chapter 8, you'll learn how to use your completed will draft to word process or type the final version of your will. Finally, continuing to follow the instructions in Chapter 8, you'll sign and have your will witnessed, which completes the will-making process.

Chapters 9 and 10 cover what happens after you've made a will, including suggestions on storing your will and the possibility of making changes to it. Finally, Chapter 11 gives information about going beyond this book, by either using other Nolo resources or hiring a lawyer. ■

Your Beneficiaries

Your beneficiaries consist of any people or organizations you choose to receive your property after you die. Clearly, deciding who will be your beneficiaries is a personal matter, one you are unlikely to need advice on. (And if you do, I'm not the one to give it, because I don't know about your personal situation and desires.)

In this chapter, I address certain basic issues and concerns that may arise even if your beneficiary situation seems clear to you at first, or even last, glance.

A. Categories of Beneficiaries

For will purposes, there are four categories of beneficiaries: primary beneficiaries, alternate beneficiaries, the beneficiary of your residuary estate and the alternate residuary beneficiary. Let's look at each of these in some detail.

1. Primary Beneficiaries

Your first choices to receive specific gifts of property are your primary beneficiaries. If you leave all your property to one person, that person is your only primary beneficiary. If you leave property to different people or organizations, you have several primary beneficiaries.

Example: *Ken wants to leave several specific gifts. He wants to leave his house, car and bank accounts to his wife, Gertrude. He wants to leave his art collection to the local museum. He wants to leave his books to the public library. Finally, he wants his daughter, Leslie, to inherit 60% of his vacation home and his son, Peter, to inherit 40%. All of these people and organizations are Ken's primary beneficiaries.*

CHARITIES AS BENEFICIARIES

You may want to leave property to a charity or a public or private organization—for example, the American Red Cross, the Greenview Battered Women's Shelter, the University of Missouri.

The organization you name need not be set up as a nonprofit, unless you wish your estate to qualify for a charitable estate tax deduction, which few readers of a basic will book need be concerned with. In fact, you can leave property to any organization you consider worthy; the only limitation is that the organization must not be set up for some illicit or illegal purpose.

2. Alternate Beneficiaries

Many people wonder what would happen if a person named in their will to receive a gift failed to survive them. Should you address this contingency in your will? For most people, the answer is "yes." They name alternate beneficiaries to receive gifts if their first choice for that gift dies before (or around the same time) they do. Doing this is sensible for a number of reasons. Perhaps you've made some gifts to older people, or relatives in poor health who may not survive you. Or maybe you just don't want to worry about redoing your will if a beneficiary happens to die before you.

Example: *Juanita leaves most of her property to her husband, Alfredo. She leaves some jewelry to her sister, Isabella. She names her son, Macito, as the alternate beneficiary for the property left to her husband. She names Isabella's daughter, Simone, as alternate beneficiary for the jewelry.*

On the other hand, some people aren't concerned about their beneficiaries dying before they do and decide not to name alternate beneficiaries. This approach is more likely when the primary beneficiaries are considerably younger than the will writer. Also, many people figure that if a beneficiary does die before they do, they'll probably have time enough to modify their will to name a new beneficiary.

On balance, I urge you to name alternate beneficiaries. It's easy to do. Chapter 7, Preparing the Draft of Your Will, will take you through that process. So, if the unexpected occurs and a beneficiary does not survive you, you'll have your will distribution plan intact.

3. Beneficiary of Your Residuary Estate

Your residuary estate consists of all property you own at your death, including property you overlooked when making your will and property that came into your hands after you made your will, except for:

- property you've specifically identified in your will that passes to primary and alternate beneficiaries you've named, and

- property that passes to people outside of your will because of other arrangements you made while you were alive, such as putting the property in a living trust, setting up a pay-on-death bank account or creating a joint tenancy ownership in the property. (I discuss these arrangements in Chapter 6, Estate Planning, Section B.)

You can, if you wish, name one sole residuary beneficiary or any number of residuary beneficiaries, possibly combining individuals and organizations, to share in your residuary estate as you specify. (See Section B, below, for more on shared gifts.)

How an individual will writer decides to distribute his or her property can vary widely. Some people leave the bulk, or even all, of their property to residuary beneficiaries. Some name specific beneficiaries for many, or even all, of their specific items of property. And, of course, there is a broad range where these two approaches are blended to suit individual needs.

4. Alternate Residuary Beneficiary

Your alternate residuary beneficiary (or beneficiaries) are—guess. That's right—whoever you name to receive your residuary estate if the residuary beneficiary (or beneficiaries) dies before you do.

Example: *Barbara makes specific gifts of cash to each of her two children. She leaves the remainder of her property—her residuary estate—to her husband, Paul. She names her children as the alternate residuary beneficiaries, to inherit in equal shares. When Barbara dies, Paul will receive everything she owns, with the exception of the money left to her children. But if Paul doesn't outlive Barbara, the children will receive their specified cash gifts plus equal shares of the residuary estate.*

B. Shared Gifts

Many people understandably want to leave the same property to be shared by more than one person. An obvious example is a parent who wants to leave all her property in equal shares to her five children. Another example is someone who wants to leave 75% of his house to his sister and 25% to his nephew. At first this may seem straightforward, but there can be lurking complexities with shared gifts.

1. Shared Gifts to Primary or Residuary Beneficiaries

The major issue here is how to clearly specify what rights each beneficiary has in the gift. The wills in this book provide that if you don't specify shares (percentages), all beneficiaries of a shared gift receive an equal share.

If you want to give unequal shares, specify that by percentage amounts. Percentages are not subject to fluctuations in the value of the gift property. By contrast, if your stock account has a current value of $100,000 and you leave $40,000 worth of the account to Suzy and $60,000 to Myron, there's going to be confusion for sure, and probably trouble, if the account value has fallen to $77,000 when you die. So to avoid this, identify the shares in any gift or your residuary estate by percentages. And of course, do make sure the percentages you leave add up to 100%.

Example: *Mariko wants to leave several shared gifts. She leaves an unimproved parcel of land to her sons, Kai and Toshiro, in equal shares. She leaves her art collection to her brother, Chiyuki (50%) and to her sisters, Yukiko (30%) and Noriko (20%). Finally, she leaves her stock portfolio to her three nephews: 50% to Kunio, 30% to Iwao and 20% to Eiji.*

Shared gifts can raise serious problems, even conflicts, about control. Suppose your house passes in equal shares to your three children. What happens if two want to sell it and one doesn't? Or take the art collection in the previous example, left by Mariko in unequal shares to her brother and two sisters. The collection is to be divided 50%, 30% and 20%. How is this determined? If all three siblings agree to sell the art collection, there shouldn't be a problem. But suppose they want to keep their portions. How do they agree on what is 20% of the art collection? Or 30%? Or 50%? Must they hire an appraiser? Will one appraiser be enough (after all, appraisal is far from a science)? And what if they all want the same artwork?

This book takes a very simple, perhaps sledgehammer, approach to questions of conflict between shared gifts. The wills in this book provide that all shared gifts must be sold, and the net proceeds distributed as the will directs, unless all beneficiaries for that gift agree in writing, after the will writer's death, that the gift need not be sold. If all agree to retain the property, they must find a mutually agreeable method for resolving valuation and any other issues.

If you want to allow one of the beneficiaries to prevent sale of a shared gift:
With a lawyer's help, you can add provisions to your will to address the issue of control over shared gifts. For instance, "The house cannot be sold unless all three of my children agree on it." But often other problems follow. If two want to sell the house, but one doesn't, who has to manage the house? Does the house have to be rented at market value? Can the child who wants to keep the house live in it? If she does, must she pay the others any rent? What happens if one child dies? Clearly, trying to address these contingencies in a will removes it from the "basic" category. Figuring out sensible ways to write a will covering these "what ifs" is a lawyer's stock and trade. But before you pay an attorney to do this, be clear you really feel it is necessary for you to resolve such questions. For many people, it makes more sense to leave shared gifts outright to the beneficiaries. If all beneficiaries agree to keep it, fine. If not, selling the property and dividing the proceeds as you've directed in your will is direct and clear.

2. Alternate Beneficiaries and Alternate Residuary Beneficiaries for Shared Gifts

Let's say you leave shared gifts, and one of the beneficiaries dies before you. Who receives the gift (assuming you didn't redo your will)? You have two options:

- You can have the surviving primary or residuary beneficiaries share the interest of any beneficiary who dies, or
- You can use your will to name one or more alternate beneficiaries for each primary or residuary beneficiary of the shared gift.

If you choose the first option (having the gift divided between surviving beneficiaries), you don't need to do anything to your will. All the will forms in this book provide that: "A deceased beneficiary's share of a shared (or residuary) gift shall be divided equally among the surviving beneficiaries of that gift, unless this will specifically provides otherwise."

Example: *John leaves a specific gift of land to be shared equally by Tony, Melinda and Biff. Tony predeceases John. When John dies, the gift will be divided equally between Melinda and Biff (unless John revised his will after Tony died).*

If you want to specify who the alternate beneficiaries should be for each primary or residuary beneficiary of a shared gift, you must simply split the shared gift in separate portions, so you can make separate specific gifts to different beneficiaries. Then name different alternate beneficiaries for each primary or residuary beneficiary.

Example: *Mike wants to leave his house to his two sons, Anthony and Travis, and his sister, Virginia. He wants each son to receive a 40% share and his sister a 20% share of the house. In the event one son does not survive him, he wants that son's share to go his child or children. If his sister predeceases him, Mike wants that 20% share to pass to Virginia's son, Malcolm. To accomplish his goals, Mike makes three separate specific gifts in his will, divided as follows:*

40% share in cabin:	*Primary beneficiary—Anthony*
	Alternate beneficiary—Anthony's children,
	Jessica and Tricia, equally
40% share in cabin:	*Primary beneficiary—Travis*
	Alternate beneficiary—Travis's son, Jason
20% share in cabin:	*Primary beneficiary—Virginia*
	Alternate beneficiary—Virginia's son, Malcolm

C. Survivorship Period

In will terms, a "survivorship period" is a defined period of time by which a beneficiary must outlive the will writer in order to legally receive property left to that beneficiary. If that beneficiary fails to survive the will writer by the set time period, the property goes to the next in line to receive it, as specified in the will.

Without a survivorship period, a beneficiary who dies shortly after you will never receive your intended gift; instead, it will end up in his or her estate. The result is that the property you'd left for a loved one to use and enjoy merely raises the dollar value of the recipient's estate, possibly increasing estate taxes and becoming subject to additional probate fees. Also, this property now passes under the terms of your beneficiary's will, rather than going to someone you've chosen.

The wills in this book impose a 45-day survivorship period on all gifts left to beneficiaries, primary, residuary or alternates.

Example: *Using a will from this book, Justine leaves her jewelry to her sister Edina. The alternate beneficiary is Justine's niece, Muriel. Justine dies; Edina dies 32 days later. Justine's jewelry goes to Muriel, because Edina didn't survive Justine by 45 days. The jewelry was never legally owned by Edina.*

Why do this book's wills impose a 45-day survivorship period, as opposed to, say, 90 days or nine days? Nolo has chosen 45 days as a sensible balance between a period that lasts for many months, needlessly tying up the estate, and one that seems so short as to run afoul of the "Why bother?" rule.

D. Simultaneous Death

Many couples, married or not, are concerned about what would happen in the unlikely event they both die at or near the same time. The possibility may be remote, but it's surely been known to happen. For example, what happens if the couple dies together in an airplane crash, a fatal car accident or a hiking disaster? However tragic such a fate, this book's will forms provide clauses that will at least clarify who will receive gifts from each person's estate.

Couples are often concerned that one spouse may briefly outlive the other, sending all the deceased spouse's property in the estate of the (briefly) surviving spouse. This can be undesirable for estate tax reasons, and also may result in a property distribution the first spouse didn't want. After all, there are no laws requiring each spouse to choose all the same beneficiaries, especially alternate or residuary ones.

The 45-day survivorship periods described in Section C, just above, are applicable to all beneficiaries, including a spouse or mate. Therefore, one spouse simply cannot inherit the other spouse's property if the survivor only lives a few minutes, or less than 45 days, beyond the first spouse to die.

Example: *Pete and Margaret each leave all their property to each other as residuary beneficiaries but have different choices for alternate residuary beneficiaries. The couple takes a ride in a hot air balloon, which explodes. Pete dies almost instantly; Margaret lingers alive for five days, then dies. Because of the 45-day survivorship period, Margaret never legally inherits Pete's property. Pete's property goes to his alternate residuary beneficiaries. Margaret's property goes to her alternate residuary beneficiaries.*

E. Imposing Limits on Your Gifts

You cannot use a will from this book to impose limits or restrictions on your gifts (aside from controls over gifts to minor children, discussed in Chapter 4, Section B). What is a limit or restriction? Any conditions or "strings" attached to the gift, such as:

- your house will go your sister after you die, and then to your children after her death
- your son is to receive money if he goes to college, or
- your vintage Barbie doll collection will go to your best friend if the dolls are in good condition. (Who is to determine if the dolls are in good condition?)

In some situations, there can be very sensible reasons for a person to want to impose limits or restrictions on a gift, but those complexities are beyond the scope of this book. Here are two common examples.

Example 1: *Eleanor, in her 50s, is in her second marriage. She has three children from her prior marriage. Her major asset is a house that she owns (the mortgage is paid off). If she dies before her husband, Peter, she wants him to be able to continue living in the house. But when he dies, she wants the house's worth to be divided equally between her three children. In this situation, Eleanor would want to create, and have her lawyer draft, what's called a "life estate" trust, allowing Peter the right to live in the house for his life, but no rights to own the house or leave it to others in his will. After Peter's death, the house would pass to Eleanor's children.*

Example 2: *Joe and LaToya have a mentally disabled son, Lamont, age 24. They each want to leave money for Lamont's benefit, but he cannot manage money himself. After both spouses die, there must be a trustee of a trust created by Joe and LaToya to manage property left for Lamont's benefit. This trust should be prepared to minimize the possibility that the principal could be consumed by a government agency in recompense for government aid Lamont receives. This type of trust is called a "special needs" trust and must be prepared by an expert in this legal area.*

Restrictions always raise complexities. There are many more reasons why someone might sensibly want to impose restrictions on a gift. My point here is simply that you can't impose any restrictions using a will from this book (beyond those imposed by the form itself, such as the 45-day survivorship period, or special property provisions for minor children). You should see an attorney before imposing any restrictions on a gift.

F. Disinheritance

Disinheritance is not a subject that typically concerns most people preparing a basic will. The word "disinheritance" has harsh, perhaps sad, overtones, since it means you've decided to exclude from your will someone very close to you, generally a family member. But sad or not, it's certainly been known to happen. Here are the state law rules and limits regarding disinheritance.

1. Spouses

In the majority of states, called "common law states," you do not have the legal right to disinherit your spouse. (See Chapter 3, Property Ownership, Section E.) In these states, to be safe, you must leave your spouse at least one-half of your estate.

The other states are "community property states," where you own half of the community property owned by you and your spouse. You can leave your half of the community property (as well as any separate property you own) to anyone you wish. A spouse in these states has no legal right to any of your property.

2. Children

In all states, you can disinherit a child, but your intent to do so must be clearly expressed in your will. The same functional result can be accomplished by leaving the child a very small amount of property. But you cannot disinherit a child simply by failing to mention that child in your will. If you don't mention a child in your will, that child generally has a legal right to some of your property. (The rules for disinheriting a child are discussed in more detail in Chapter 4, Children, Section C3.)

3. Disinheriting Other People

With the exception of spouses, and children not expressly disinherited in your will, you can disinherit anyone else you want to by simply not naming them in the will. Actually, the word "disinherit" isn't really correct here, since no one other than a spouse and children has any inherent right to your property (unless you've made a valid contract to leave someone some property in your will). So omitting a person—from "next of kin" to anyone else—from your will isn't disinheriting that person, because they weren't entitled to inherit in the first place.

You may have heard that some lawyers recommend leaving $1 to relatives or friends you want to disinherit. Is doing this legally necessary? No, and there's no sensible reason to do it, either. Why mention a relative or friend in your will only to leave them $1, when they otherwise wouldn't be entitled to anything? Tracking down such beneficiaries, and getting them to sign a receipt form, can be a real hassle for your executor, all to hand over one buck.

If you think someone might contest your will: If you suspect that, after your death, one or another of your relatives might contest your will, be prudent and see a lawyer. You'll want to make sure you've done all you can to discourage a will contest, or that your intentions will prevail if a contest does occur.

G. If You Want to Explain Your Decisions

The wills in this book have been prepared with painstaking attention, to allow you to make a legal and unambiguous will. They do not contain space for you to explain to your beneficiaries why you made your gifts, or to express other sentiments and emotions.

Fortunately, there is a way you can have your final say about personal matters without risking your will's legal validity or integrity. You can write a letter to accompany your will expressing your thoughts to those who survive you. Your letter must expressly state that you do not intend this letter to modify or affect your will in any way, and that you know this letter is solely a personal statement of your feelings and emotions.

Writing a letter to your loved ones to explain why you wrote your will as you did—and knowing they will read your reasoning after your death—can give you some peace of mind during life about your property distribution. Writing this type of letter is explained further in Chapter 8, Preparing Your Final Will, Section F. ■

CHAPTER 3

Property Ownership

As you know, you use a will to leave your property to others after your death. Obviously, you can't leave property by will unless it belongs to you in the first place. For many people, there are no real questions about property ownership. "Hey, I [or I and my spouse] own a house, household furnishings, clothes, a car, a checking account, a small savings account and a smaller mutual stock fund—what else do I need to know?" In this instance, nothing at all. For people with small estates, or those who keep their property information in their heads, knowing what property they own is easy.

Further, if you plan to leave all of your property to one person or as a shared gift to two or more persons, you don't need a detailed list of all of your property, no matter how complicated your holdings. Similarly, if you plan to make only one, or few, individual gifts and leave the rest of your property to one person, you shouldn't need to spend a lot of time cataloging what you own.

However, many people do need to at least check out one or more issues regarding property, especially if they co-own property with anyone, including a spouse. Some readers may be surprised to find that they don't own what they think they do. Most will learn they have no problem at all here. But do read on, because you need to be clear about your property situation to create a will using this book.

This chapter helps you:
- learn some basic legal rules about property ownership, so you can make sure you own the property you believe you do, and
- inventory your property, if you need to.

DEFINITION OF "PROPERTY"

I have already defined property (in Chapter 1) as being anything you own. Lawyers make various distinctions between types of property. "Real property" means real estate, land and any buildings permanently attached to that land. "Personal property" means all other types of property, from lipstick to tens of thousands of dollars in an investment.

Happily for your will-writing purposes, you don't need to bother with different classifications of property. Any item you own is your property. It may have market value, like a house or car, or it may have none, like family photos or treasured letters (from someone who's not famous). It's all your property, and you may distribute each item as you wish.

A. Basic Rules for Giving Away Property

Here I cover some basic rules about leaving property by will that people sometimes have questions about. We'll get to state law regarding property ownership shortly, in Section D.

Rule 1: Your State's Laws Govern All or Most of Your Property

Generally, the laws of the state where you legally reside apply to all property you own. If you are married, this can be extremely important, because state laws in most states give your spouse certain rights to your property, no matter what you provide in your will. (See discussion in Section E.) Otherwise, state laws normally have no impact on will distribution. However, in certain instances, laws of another state or country apply:

- *real estate located in another state.* Each state's laws govern all real estate located within that state, and

- *property located in another country.* Each country has its own laws governing all property (real estate, bank accounts and all other items) that exists within its borders.

The state of your legal residence (where you legally live) is where you make your home. You can have only one legal residence. If you divide up the year by living in two or more states or you are temporarily residing outside the United States, choose as your state of residence the state in which you are the most rooted—for instance, where you:

- are registered to vote
- register your motor vehicles
- own real estate or other valuable property
- have checking, savings and other investment accounts, or
- maintain a business.

If you live overseas temporarily because you are in the Armed Services, your residence will be the Home of Record you declared to the military authorities.

Rule 2:   Only Property You Own at the Time of Death Is Passed by Will

Few people try to leave property they've never owned. Problems can arise when a will writer leaves a specific item of property that was sold, given away or lost between the time the will was drafted and the will writer's death. What happens in this case? That's easy. If a specific gift is made in a will, and that property is no longer owned by the will writer when he or she dies, the gift is void. That's it.

Example: *Al has a classic MG convertible that he's lovingly (and expensively) restored and owned for decades. In his will, he specifically leaves the car to his daughter, Darlene. But several years after writing his will, Al experiences some tight financial times and sells the MG. When Al dies, Darlene obviously won't get the car. Further, she has no right to the dollar value of the car.*

Moral: Be sure you keep your will up-to-date regarding your property. But note that if you leave all your property to one person, or divide it all among several, there's no specific gift that could be later voided, so there is far less chance of your beneficiaries feeling disappointed.

Rule 3:   You Can't Use a Will to Give Away Property That Will Automatically Be Transferred Upon Your Death

It's common to arrange for some property to be passed automatically to others upon the owner's death, thereby avoiding probate. This property cannot be given away by will. For example, there are many significant items of property for which you can name beneficiaries on the ownership documents, including many retirement plans, such as IRAs, 401(k)s and profit-sharing plans. (If you don't know what one, or all, of these are, don't worry. That means you don't have one.) Also included here are insurance policies, certain types of bank accounts (called pay-on-death accounts) and securities (stocks and bonds) held under the Securities Transfer on Death Act.

Example: *Jordan takes out a life insurance policy and names his daughter, Carmel, as the beneficiary, to receive the proceeds when he dies. Carmel will receive the proceeds directly after Jordan dies; the money won't pass through Jordan's will or the probate court. Even if Jordan names different beneficiaries for the life insurance proceeds in his will, this designation would be meaningless and ineffective; Carmel will still get the money.*

Other legal methods of transferring property at death include well-known probate avoidance methods such as living trusts and joint tenancy. All major transfer methods are discussed in Chapter 6, Estate Planning.

Rule 4: You May Not Be Able to Give Away Co-Owned Business Property by Will

You need to check the ownership agreement of any shared business to see what your rights are to leave your interest by will. Often the other owners have the right to buy out a deceased owner's interest, using a predetermined valuation method. Of course, even if the other owners have the option to buy out your share of the business, they won't have to exercise this option unless it's a very unusual agreement.

If you can't leave your business interest, you can still leave whatever money the surviving owners pay for your share by your will, so that the money goes to whomever you want to receive it. Because you can't know in advance what the buy-out price will be, don't leave specific dollar amounts of it to beneficiaries. You should simply leave all of your interest to one beneficiary, or percentages of your interest to different beneficiaries.

Rule 5: Property Loans and Encumbrances Become the Responsibility of the Beneficiaries

Using the wills in this book, your beneficiary for property with money owed on it, such as a car with a loan on it or a house with a mortgage, receives it subject to the encumbrance. In other words, if you don't own something free and clear, neither will your beneficiaries. If you want your estate to pay off the encumbrance, use another Nolo will writing resource. See Chapter 11, Going Further, Section A.

Rule 6:   You Can't Leave Money or Property to Pets Outright

Pets aren't people, and they can't legally own money or property (even if they sometimes act like they do), so you can't leave them money or property in your will. You also can't use your will to put binding requirements on your pet's care, such as requiring certain grooming procedures or a certain type of food. You can, however, give your pets away in your will. It's common to leave a pet to a friend or family member who's willing to care for it, perhaps with money to help pay for the pet's care. You also might wish to write a separate letter setting out details of how you'd like the beneficiary to care for your pet.

PETS AS BENEFICIARIES OF A TRUST

In the following states, you can name a pet as a beneficiary of a trust:
Alaska, Arizona, California, Missouri, Montana, New Mexico, New York, North Carolina, Tennessee.

In a pet trust, you name a trustee with responsibility for taking care of the pet, using trust funds. Obviously, the beneficiary of the trust, the pet, cannot enforce the trust terms. So pet trusts are called "honorary trusts," or ones "binding on the conscience of the trustee."

You'll need to see a lawyer to prepare a trust naming a pet as beneficiary.

B. Taking Stock of Your Property

People who are preparing a basic will usually have a good idea of what they own, without needing to make an extensive property inventory. Many readers won't need to inventory their property at all, especially if they are leaving all of it to one or just a few persons. But before you prepare your will, it's wise to pause and check to be sure there are no special items of property you might have overlooked. This is particularly important if you want to leave some special or sentimental items to specific beneficiaries. For example, maybe you have a collection of special heirlooms you want to give to a family member or close friend. Nor is it just expensive items you may care the most about; certain photos, journals or mementos of friendship may be equally precious.

It won't take much time for you to go through the "Property You May Want to Leave by Will" list on the next page to help jog your memory about what property you own.

If your property ownership is complex and valuable: If you believe an in-depth inventory would be helpful, you should seek help beyond this book.

PROPERTY YOU MAY WANT TO LEAVE BY WILL

Real Estate (land and items permanently attached to land)

Agricultural land	Duplex	Time-share
Boat/marina dock space	House	Undeveloped land
Condo	Mobile home	Vacation house
Co-op	Rental property	

Personal Property (property other than real estate)

Animals	Computer equipment	Safe deposit contents
Antiques	Copyrights, patents,	Securities:
Appliances	trademarks	Bonds
Art	Electronic equipment	Commodities
Bank and cash accounts:	Family heirlooms	Mutual funds
Certificates of deposit	Furniture	Stocks
Checking accounts	Hobbies	Sentimental items
Money market funds	Household furnishings	Small businesses
Savings accounts	Inheritances	Sports equipment
Bicycles	Jewelry	Tools
Books	Letters, documents, papers	U.S. bills, notes and bonds
Business interests	Medals, awards, trophies	Vehicles, boats, aircraft:
Cameras, photographic and	Musical instruments	Airplanes
video equipment	Pets	Automobiles
China, crystal, silver	Photographs	Boats
Clothing, furs	Precious metals	Motorcycles
Coins, stamps	Promissory notes, debts	Motor homes/RVs
Collectibles (records, dolls,	owed to you	Watches
baseball cards, etc.)	Religious items, artifacts	Wedding and engagement
	Royalties	rings

C. The Beneficiary Worksheet

Once you've pinned down what property you own, you may find the Beneficiary Worksheet in the Appendix helpful for deciding who gets what. You can use it to work out who your beneficiaries are and exactly what each one receives. The Beneficiary Worksheet can be useful in a variety of situations:

- Readers who simply aren't sure how they want to divide up their property can rough out (in pencil) their options and make decisions as they go along.

- The Beneficiary Worksheet can help you organize your will writing choices so you don't overlook important items of property or accidentally forget any beneficiaries.

- Some readers own a variety of property and wish to divide it among a number of people and organizations. The Beneficiary Worksheet can be a handy place for organizing that data.

Let me conclude by reminding you that many readers' situations are clear enough so they'll have no need for the Beneficiary Worksheet. Don't use it if it isn't helpful.

YOU DON'T NEED TO USE LEGAL TERMINOLOGY TO LEAVE PROPERTY BY WILL

Some people ask, "Don't I need to use some technical, legal language to describe property I leave in my will?" The answer is no. There are no legal requirements governing how you identify your property. I discuss this matter now because I want to reassure you that when you're ready to prepare your will, you won't be burdened with legalese when it comes to describing your property. (This matter is further discussed in Chapter 7, Preparing the Draft of Your Will.)

Here's some more good news. If you leave all your property to one person (or all your property to multiple beneficiaries in a shared gift), you won't even have to bother describing it.

If you leave a number of items of property to one or several beneficiaries, that property must be described sufficiently so that those beneficiaries, and the person you've named to carry out your will, are clear about what you meant. All that is needed to achieve this is a plain, commonsense description of the property. Describing your property in your will won't be hard and is certainly no stumbling block to preparing your will yourself.

D. Types of Property Ownership

Here I briefly cover the basic legal forms of property ownership. This section should provide sufficient information to alert you if you may have a complicated property ownership situation. If you are married, you'll also need to read Section E of this chapter, which covers property rights between husband and wife.

1. Outright Ownership

The simplest form of ownership exists when you are the only owner—that is, you do not share ownership and you are not married. For the purpose of making your will, you are the sole owner—even if a lender has some legal ownership in the property until you pay off the loan, as is true with car notes and mortgages.

2. Tenancy in Common

In a tenancy in common, all owners have equal rights to use the property. Ownership shares may be equal, but it is also possible to arrange for unequal shares by deed or written contract. Each co-owner is free to transfer, by will, his or her interest to anyone she or he chooses.

Tenancy in common is the most common way for unmarried people to own property together. Married couples also can use this form of co-ownership, but more often choose joint tenancy or tenancy by the entirety, discussed below in Sections D3 and D4.

3. Joint Tenancy with Right of Survivorship

Any two (or more) people can own property—typically real estate or a bank account—in joint tenancy with right of survivorship. When one of them dies, his or her share automatically goes to the surviving owner. *A joint tenant cannot use a will to leave his or her share of joint tenancy property to someone else.*

Example: *Avram is a widower. He and his brother Sid own a house together. Avram wants to leave large gifts to his son, Ben, and his daughter, Freida. He plans to leave Ben a large gift of cash. At first, he considers leaving Freida his half of the house. Then Avram looks at the deed to the house and realizes that the property is held in joint tenancy, so Avram's brother automatically owns his half if Avram dies first. If Avram uses his will to leave his share of the house to Freida, she won't be entitled to it, meaning Ben would get cash and Freida would get nothing. Avram instead decides to leave both Ben and Freida cash gifts.*

SIMULTANEOUS DEATH OF JOINT TENANTS

If all joint tenants die simultaneously, no one owner has survived any of the others. In that case, each joint tenant's interest in the property passes by their will. Under the wills in this book, in this situation, a person's joint tenancy interest would become part of the residuary estate and pass to the named residuary beneficiary or alternate.

Example: Sylvia and Henry are married and own their home in joint tenancy. They are both killed in a boating disaster. Sylvia's one-half interest in the joint tenancy property passes to her residuary beneficiary. Henry's one-half goes to his residuary beneficiary. (If Sylvia and Henry were the other's residuary beneficiary, each one's property would go to his or her alternate residuary beneficiary.)

Joint tenancies with right of survivorship are created by specific words in an ownership document, such as a real estate deed or bank account certificate. To find out whether you own property in joint tenancy, check the document for the words "joint tenants," "joint tenancy" or "with the right of survivorship." A few states require the document to read "joint tenancy with the right of survivorship," and Oregon, for example, requires the words "tenancy in common with the right of survivorship" to set up this kind of joint ownership.

Sometimes owners decide to change ownership of property from joint tenancy to tenancy in common in order to leave their interests to someone other than the surviving joint tenant(s). In most all states, it's relatively easy for one owner to accomplish this change. Indeed, in most states, transfers out of joint tenancy into another form of co-ownership can be done even if the other joint tenant objects. You need to check with some authority, such as a title company or a real estate lawyer, to determine the precise mechanics required.

Example: *Avram (from the previous example) decides he wants his share of his house to go to his daughter, and not to his brother Sid. Avram prepares the documents required in his state to take the house out of joint tenancy with Sid and place it in tenancy in common. Avram and Sid continue to each own 50% of the house, but Avram may now leave his interest to his daughter, by will, without trouble.*

STATES THAT HAVE RESTRICTED OR ABOLISHED JOINT TENANCY

The following states have limited or abolished joint tenancy. If you live in one of these states and you have a joint tenancy ownership document, check with a lawyer to see what you've really got.

Alaska	No joint tenancy in real estate, except for husband and wife.
Ohio	Owner agreement must expressly state "for their joint lives, remainder to the survivor of them."
Oregon	Technically, no joint tenancy, but the right of survivorship may be created by express agreement between joint owners. Transfers to husband and wife are considered tenancies by the entirety.
Tennessee	Technically, no joint tenancy, but the right of survivorship may be created by express agreement between joint owners. Transfers to husband and wife are considered tenancies by the entirety.
Texas	Technically, no joint tenancy, but the right of survivorship may be created by written agreement between joint owners.

4. Tenancy by the Entirety

This form of ownership is basically the same as joint tenancy with right of survivorship discussed above but is limited to married couples. The phrase "tenancy by the entirety" or "as tenants by the entirety" must appear in the deed. When one spouse dies, the entire interest in the property automatically goes to the other. Before tenancy by the entirety property can be changed to some other form of property ownership, both spouses must agree to the change.

STATES WITH TENANCY BY THE ENTIRETY OWNERSHIP

*Alaska	Maryland	Oklahoma
Arkansas	Massachusetts	*Oregon
Delaware	Michigan	Pennsylvania
District of Columbia	Mississippi	Rhode Island
Florida	Missouri	Tennessee
Hawaii	New Jersey	Vermont
*Illinois	*New York	Virginia
*Indiana	*North Carolina	Wyoming
Kentucky	**Ohio	

*Allows tenancy by the entirety only for real estate.

**Created before 4/4/85

E. Marital Property

If you're not married: If you're single, divorced or widowed, skip the rest of this chapter. But if you're married or in the process of getting a divorce, you'll need to read this section.

The great majority of married people leave all or most of their property to the surviving spouse at death. For them, the nuances of state marital property law are not relevant. Even if you want to leave some gifts to other family members, friends or institutions, your marital property situation will usually be simple, as long as you're leaving at least one-half of your property to your spouse.

If you plan to leave substantial amounts to someone instead of, or in addition to, your spouse, the picture becomes more complicated. Questions of which spouse owns what property may then become important, unless your spouse consents to your plan for property disposition, as is most often true when older spouses leave property directly to their adult children.

YOUR MARITAL STATUS AND YOUR WILL

Most readers' marital status is clear: they know if they're married or they're not. But in some situations, a person's marital status, for will-writing purposes, isn't so clear. Your marital status could affect how and to whom you can leave your property. For example, if you're separated but not yet divorced, your estranged spouse may have a right to inherit one-third to one-half of what you own.

If you're in the process of divorcing, or are planning to marry, it's fine to make a will now. But make sure you write your will over again after your marital status changes. (See Chapter 10, Changing or Revoking Your Will, Section A.)

If you are unsure whether you are married or single according to law, here are some tips:

- *Separation or pending divorce or annulment.* You remain legally married until a court issues a formal decree of divorce or annulment, signed by a judge. This is true even if you and your spouse have filed for divorce or annulment, are legally separated as declared in a legal document or live apart for an extended time.
- *Common law marriages.* In a number of states, an unmarried woman and man automatically become legally married if they live together and either hold themselves out to the public as being married or actually intend to be married to one another. Common law marriages are recognized in: Alabama, Colorado, the District of Columbia, Georgia (created before 1/1/97), Idaho (created before 1/1/96), Iowa, Kansas, Montana, New Hampshire (for inheritance purposes only), Ohio (created before 10/10/91), Oklahoma, Pennsylvania, Rhode Island, South Carolina, Texas and Utah. The common law marriage will still be valid even if the spouses later move to a different state. There is no such thing as a common law divorce; a formal divorce proceeding is necessary to end a marriage.
- *Same sex marriages.* No state legally recognizes marriages between people of the same sex, even where a religious ceremony has been performed.

In this section, I briefly cover the main issues of marital property. I don't go into these issues in depth because few users of this book face such concerns. If after reading this section you think you may have a more complex marital partnership problem, turn to Chapter 11, Going Further.

Fortunately, learning the basics of marital property law is not difficult. For the purpose of deciding what is in your estate when you die, states are divided into two types: community property states and common law property states.

COMMUNITY PROPERTY STATES	COMMON LAW STATES
Arizona	All other states
California	
Idaho	
Nevada	
New Mexico	
Texas	
Washington	
Wisconsin*	

*While Wisconsin is not technically a community property state, it changed its marital property law on January 1, 1986, to resemble those found in community property states. This law covers all property owned at a person's death, including any property that was accumulated before 1986.

1. Community Property States

In community property states, what you own and can leave by will consists of:

- your own separate property, and

- one-half of the community property you and your spouse own together.

Now let's look at both forms of property ownership possible in community property states.

a. Separate Property

In community property states, a spouse's separate property is:

- all property acquired prior to marriage

- income earned from previously-owned property, if the spouse who earned it keeps it separate—except in Washington, where this type of income is always community property

- gifts or inheritances received during marriage, if directed to only one spouse (wedding gifts are community property)

- property that, despite originally being classified as community property, is converted into separate property by gift or agreement (which must be in writing in some states), and

- property acquired after legal separation.

b. Community Property

The system of community property derived from Spanish law, which viewed both partners in a marriage as contributing equally, no matter whose name was on a paycheck, deed, bank account or other legal document (rather a contemporary view).

In community property states, community property is owned in equal shares by a married couple—that is, each spouse owns 50%. Community property consists of:

- income from work performed by either spouse during marriage

- property and earnings acquired from community income

- gifts made to both spouses

- property that, despite originally being classified as separate property, is deliberately turned into community property by the spouses. This commonly occurs when one spouse makes a gift of separate property to the community, such as transferring the title of a separately owned home into both spouses' names, and

- separate property that is so mixed up with community property ("commingled," in legalese) that one can no longer distinguish the two. In this case, the property becomes all community property. This can easily happen when income from separate property is put in a shared bank account.

c. Property That Is Difficult to Categorize

Normally, classifying property as community or separate is easy enough, but in some situations, it can be a close call. Here I merely indicate several potential problem areas that may arise. (If you have complications in one of these areas, see Chapter 11, Going Further.)

- *Businesses.* A family-owned business can create complications, especially if it was owned before marriage by one spouse and expanded during the marriage. The key is to figure out whether an increased value of the business is community or separate property. Of course, if you plan to leave your share of the business to your spouse, or in a way your spouse approves of, you have no practical problem.

- *Money judgment for personal injuries.* Usually, personal injury awards won in a lawsuit are the separate property of the spouse receiving them, but not always. Indeed, there is no easy way to characterize this type of property.

- *Some pensions.* Pensions gained from community income received by a spouse during a marriage generally are considered to be community property. This community property rule applies to military pensions. However, some federal pensions—such as Railroad Retirement benefits and Social Security retirement benefits—are not considered community property because federal law deems them to be the separate property of the employee earning them.

- *Debts.* Generally, either spouse's debts for food, shelter and other necessities of life are considered to be incurred on behalf of the marriage and must be paid from the couple's community property. Each spouse, however, is individually responsible for paying personal debts. Unfortunately, the line between individual and community debts is often far from clear.

d. Rules for Leaving Community Property

You can use your will to leave your half of community property and all your separate property to whomever you want to have it, unless:

- you have arranged to transfer the property by another method (see Chapter 6, Estate Planning, Section B)

- the property has a separate designation of beneficiaries, as is common for pay-on-death bank accounts, retirement plans and life insurance contracts, or

- the property is restricted from transfer by a contract—for example, a partnership agreement that restricts how you can leave your share.

2. Common Law States

To repeat, common law property states are all states other than Arizona, California, Idaho, Nevada, New Mexico, Texas, Washington and Wisconsin.

If you live in a common law property state, the property you own individually consists of:

- all property you purchased with your separate property or separate income, and

- property you own separately in your name, if it has a title slip, deed or other legal ownership document.

In common law states, the key to ownership for many types of valuable property, whether you are married or not, is whose name is on the title. For example, if you earn or inherit money to buy a house, and title is taken in both your name and your spouse's, you both own the house. If your spouse earns the money, but you take title in your name alone, you own it. If the property has no title document, such as a computer or other electronic equipment, the person whose income or property is used to pay for it owns it. If joint income is used, ownership is shared between spouses.

a. Separate Property

A spouse's separate property is property held in his or her name. Thus, if both spouses pay for something, but only one spouse's name is on the ownership document, that person is sole owner of the property.

b. Marital Property

In common law property states, marital property is property that both spouses own together. This consists of:

- property held in both spouses' names, and
- property either or both spouses purchased with income or the proceeds of the sale of property held in both spouses' names.

c. Rules for Leaving Marital Property

The laws of common law states protect a spouse from being disinherited by the other spouse. The details of such laws vary from state to state, but for our purposes, one general rule applies. You *must* leave your spouse at least 50% of (the value of) all your property.

If you want to leave your spouse less than 50% of your property: Unless you plan to leave your spouse at least 50% of your separate property and your share of marital property combined, this book is not for you. Use another Nolo resource or consult a lawyer. (See Chapter 11, Going Further.)

You are free to give away the balance of your property that is not going to your spouse (if any) however you want to, unless:

- the property has a separate designation of beneficiaries—as is common for pay-on-death bank accounts, retirement plans and life insurance contracts
- you have arranged to transfer the property by living trust, joint tenancy or another estate planning method, or
- the property is restricted from transfer by a contract—for example, a partnership agreement that restricts you from giving away your share. ■

CHAPTER 4

Children

Being a parent may be what motivated you to make your will. Most parents of minor children (under age 18) are understandably concerned about what will happen to their children if disaster strikes and the parents die unexpectedly. In this chapter, I explain how to make specific arrangements in your will for care of your minor children should a tragedy result in no parent being available. This involves two separate, although often related, concerns:

- who will care for your minor children, and

- who will manage money and other property you and others leave them. (How much you leave them is entirely up to you, and I offer no advice on that.)

In your will, you should name an adult, or adults, to handle both functions.

A. Naming a Personal Guardian

The adult you name to have custody of your children if you and the other parent (if there is one) die while your children are minors is called the children's personal guardian. This person is responsible for raising your children, with all that entails. Usually this person is also responsible for handling any money you've left for your children's benefit, but this, as I discuss in Section B, below, is not mandatory.

You nominate your choice for personal guardian in your will. You do not nominate your spouse, because he or she will automatically continue to have custody. You are nominating a person to take over only if neither spouse is alive. However, if you don't want the other parent to gain custody, or if that parent isn't available, you'll need to name someone else as your first choice for personal guardian, as I discuss below. Usually people nominate an alternate personal guardian, to be sure this role is filled if their first choice can't do the job.

Your choice of personal guardian is not automatically legally binding. Should the need arise, the final decision of who will serve as your children's personal guardian will be made by a judge, deciding in "the children's best interest." If the other parent is deceased, has disappeared or has completely abandoned the child, the judge must decide which other adult can best raise the child. Fortunately, in uncontested cases (as most are), a court almost always confirms the parent's choice of guardian. But if you think your choice might be contested, you should see a lawyer to do all you can in advance to have your desires prevail if it ever comes to a legal battle.

1. Choosing a Personal Guardian

For parents with minor children, choosing a personal guardian is obviously a vitally important decision. Many people with minor children know before beginning the will writing process who they want to take care of their children—or, at least, are able to quickly reach a decision. When choosing a personal guardian (and alternate personal guardian), do remember the obvious: You can't "draft" someone to parent your kids. Be sure any person you name is ready, willing and able to do the job.

The wills provided in this book allow only one person to be named as personal guardian and one person as alternate personal guardian for all of a parent's minor children. While it is legally permissible to name co-guardians, this is normally a poor idea because of the possibility that the co-guardians will later disagree or go separate ways. Also, you cannot name different personal guardians for different children using these wills, because that requires a more complex will form and perhaps also an explanation in a written document of the reasons for your decisions.

If possible, each parent should name the same personal guardian and alternate. In case of simultaneous death of the parents, you surely don't want to leave a conflict regarding who will raise your kids.

More complex personal guardianship situations: Some parents want more choice in appointing personal guardians, and for any of a variety of reasons want to name different personal guardians for different children or explain the reasons for the choices of personal guardian(s). See Chapter 11, Going Further, Section A, for other Nolo resources covering these issues.

2. If One Parent Dies

If you die before your children's other parent, that other parent normally has the legal right to assume sole custody. This applies to biological and adoptive parents ("adoptive" refers to people who have legally adopted a child through a court proceeding), but not people functioning as step-parents.

For many parents, it is comforting to know that the other parent will be available to bring up the children. But what if you are strongly opposed to the other parent gaining custody? There's no one-size-fits-all answer here. If the other parent has been involved with the children, she or he will probably gain custody. Judges are very reluctant to take custody away from a biological or adoptive parent, unless that parent is proven in court to be clearly unsuitable for parenting.

A parent's desire to prevent the other parent from gaining custody, however well-founded, does not usually determine what happens. Children aren't property, so they can't be left to someone by will (or any other means). However, if it can be proven that the other parent has abandoned the children, or has neglected them for some time, a judge may decide against giving that parent custody. The best a custodial parent can do, while he or she is still living, is prepare as well as possible for a potential court fight. Preparation can include writing a statement as to exactly why someone other than the non-custodian parent would be the best guardian for the child, and having witnesses capable and willing to testify on this point in court. Dealing with this is beyond the scope of this book, and usually requires a lawyer's help.

B. Managing Minors' Property

Let's start with a basic legal rule: Minors cannot legally own property (including money) outright, free of adult supervision, beyond a minimal amount—in the $2,500 to $5,000 range, depending on the state. For parents of minor children, this means you need to arrange for an adult to handle valuable property that your children own or inherit. A will is the standard method for making arrangements to handle minors' property.

If you do not provide for this management in your will, and it becomes necessary, a judge will do what you failed to do. An expensive, public and time-consuming court process for appointment of a property guardian for your children will be necessary. The costs will come out of the children's property, usually money you've left them. The court will supervise, on an ongoing basis, how the court-appointed guardian manages and spends the money.

In writing your will, you'll have the opportunity to address two different categories of property your minor children may receive:

- *You, the parent, may wish to leave money and other property to your children in your will.* Whether you leave your minor children property directly or you name them as alternate beneficiaries, as many young parents do, you need to arrange for adult management for this property.

- *After you die, your minor children might receive property from other sources.* Your children may receive property ranging from gifts from other relatives to the child's own earnings. Also included here are life insurance proceeds or retirement plans, where you named your children as beneficiaries. Some adult will have to take charge of all these types of property if legally owned by your children.

The wills in this book that include provisions for minor children (Forms 1, 3 and 5) address both of these issues, allowing you to:

- set up what's called a children's trust for any property you leave your minor children by will, and

- appoint a property guardian to manage any other property the children receive before they are 18.

Why two methods? A children's trust is preferable to a property guardian for property you leave to your children by will, because it will normally operate free of court supervision. But a children's trust does not cover property your minor children might receive from other sources. By naming a property guardian in your will, you've ensured that you have chosen an adult to manage all property received by your children outside your will, even though this person must be approved and supervised by the court.

1. Children's Trusts

A children's trust, which is valid in all states, is a legal entity you create as part of your will. The trust merely exists on paper while you live; it only becomes operational upon your death.

A children's trust is included in each of this book's will forms that are designed for use by parents of minor children (Forms 1, 3 and 5). The trusts here have been carefully drafted and tested over time in other Nolo will products. To create a children's trust in your will, all you need do is fill in the correct information where it's called for, as explained precisely in Chapter 7, Preparing the Draft of Your Will.

In creating the trust, you appoint an adult as trustee, to have the responsibility of managing property you've left to your minor child or children in the trust. You also appoint a successor trustee in case your first choice can't serve.

The will forms in this book allow you to create a separate trust for each minor child. You must, however, name only one trustee for all trusts. Each child's trust ends when that child becomes 35, unless you choose to specify a different age, between 18 and 35, for that trust to end. Age 35 is the absolute cut-off age for each child to receive his or her property, because these trusts are primarily minor's trusts and are not designed for the lifetime management of property. Age 35 seemed like the most sensible dividing line between "young adults" and "fully mature adults" (or, youth and middle age).

MORE COMPLEX CHILDREN'S TRUSTS

For minors with complicated needs or problems, you need an attorney to draft a trust. The basic children's trusts in this book's will forms are not designed for unique situations. Specifically, an expert lawyer must draft a trust intended to:

- provide for management of trust property beyond age 35 for a person who's bad with money or has other personal habits that may impede sound financial management beyond young adulthood (called a "spendthrift trust"), or

- meet a disadvantaged beneficiary's special needs. A physical, mental or developmental disability will likely require management customized to the beneficiary's circumstances, both to best aid the beneficiary and to preserve the trust property, while assuring that the beneficiary continues to qualify for government benefits (called a "special needs" trust).

The trustee has authority to spend as much of each child's trust income and principal as he or she deems necessary for the child's "health, support, education and maintenance." This is clearly a major responsibility. The trustee must be sufficiently involved with the child, or children, to know what each needs financially. Thus, the job of a trustee can involve considerable amounts of work, especially if he or she must manage a child's trust property for many years.

Deciding how to allocate money may be more difficult for the trustee than, say, handing out jelly beans. The trustee must decide what is necessary and sensible for the child. Expensive sneakers? ("Everybody wears them.") Expensive...whatever. ("Everybody has one.") Although the task may not be easy, if you pick someone with integrity and common sense, your children's property will probably be in good hands.

Normally, the trustee's main responsibilities—beyond direct concern with the children—are to act honestly and manage each child's trust competently. This usually means investing the trust principal conservatively, keeping good financial records, filing annual trust state and federal income tax returns and using the trust income (and invading the principal, if necessary) to provide for the children's needs.

The trustee is not normally subject to court supervision. If you have confidence in your trustee, this is fine. There's simply no reason to waste time and money on court proceedings when a trustee can manage fine without that.

You may name any adults you want to as trustee and successor trustee of your children's trust. A parent does not inherently have the authority to serve as trustee of the other parent's children's trust. If you want the children's other biological parent to be trustee of property you leave directly to your children, you need to name him or her as the trustee. If you name the other parent as initial trustee, it's important to name a successor trustee to serve if both parents die together.

If you name someone other than the other parent as trustee and successor trustee, should this be the same person you name as the children's personal guardian? Often it's desirable to keep all responsibility for the children unified. But if your choice for personal guardian simply cannot handle money well (however loving he or she is), you might choose to name someone else to manage the property you've left for your children.

The adult you name as trustee should be sensible about managing money. You don't, for example, want someone to gamble (excuse me, "invest") in risky stocks, oil futures or currency. But don't worry about financial expertise. You simply want someone who knows the basics of commonsense finance, who's savvy enough to put money in a secure money market fund and can balance a checkbook.

Most important is your trust in the person, as your children may be dependent on this person's kindness and judgment at least as much as on his or her financial sense. Choose whoever you feel can do the best job of serving the real needs of your children, and, once again, who is willing to do the job.

Your choice for trustee and any successor trustee should be at least 18 years of age (21 years of age if you live in Indiana). If possible, the trustee and successor trustee should live in your state, or geographically close; someone who lives far away may have problems managing a trust.

INSURANCE TO BENEFIT YOUR CHILDREN

Many insurance companies will pay proceeds directly to a children's trust created by a will. You simply complete a form, where you name the trust as beneficiary of the policy. However, a minority of life insurance companies are reluctant to allow a trust to be beneficiary of a policy when the trust will only exist in the future (when you die). So check with your insurance company and see what they'll permit. If your insurance company won't allow you to leave the proceeds to a children's trust, you'll have to leave them directly to your children, to be managed by the property guardian.

Another approach is to create a living trust, which goes into effect immediately, and name the living trust as beneficiary of your insurance policy, with your minor children named as beneficiaries in the living trust for any proceeds from that policy. (See Chapter 6, Estate Planning, Section B.)

a. Setting Up Trusts for Minors Who Aren't Your Children

You may find it appropriate to use a children's trust for minors other than your own children. For example, if you are a grandparent and want to leave property to a grandchild, you may wish to use a children's trust and name one parent of that child as trustee. This works well in situations where you have only one son or daughter with children. If you have grandchildren from more than one child, this method won't work, however, and you'll need a more sophisticated will-drafting resource. (See Chapter 11, Going Further, Section A.)

You also can leave property to someone else's minor children using the trusts from this book, but remember—you may choose only one trustee for all. This means that it's almost always wiser to leave property for other children's benefit outright to the children's parent(s), trusting they'll use it for their children. If you want to do that, you should prepare a letter to accompany your will, stating how you want that parent to use the money for the child. This letter won't be legally binding, but should carry considerable moral/ethical weight. (See Chapter 8, Preparing Your Final Will, Section F, on explanatory letters with a will.)

2. The Property Guardian

In your will, you can nominate a property guardian (and alternate) to manage any property your minor children acquire that isn't managed by some other method (such as a children's trust). Your minor children might receive property from a variety of sources—from a gift from an aunt or uncle, or earn money from playing in a rock band. If you don't name a property guardian and your minor children receive property of significant value outside of your will, a court will usually have to step in and appoint a guardian to manage the property under court supervision until the children turn 18. The guardian a court appoints could be a crony concerned with maximizing his or her fees, not serving your children's best interests.

Here are some rules for choosing your children's property guardian:

- Name only one property guardian and one alternate for all your children.

- If you want the surviving parent to become the property guardian, you should name that person as your first choice, since if a child inherits or receives property, it's not automatic that the surviving spouse becomes the property guardian. You then name an alternate in case your spouse can't do the job.

- Select someone you trust implicitly, and make sure he or she is willing to do the job.

- If you've created a children's trust in your will, the property guardian is very likely to be the same person you named as trustee of your children's trust. If you trust that person to handle property you leave for your children, there's normally no need to name someone else to manage other property your children may acquire.

The wills in this book provide that no bond is required of the property guardian. A bond provides a financial guarantee that your children's property would be reimbursed should the property guardian mismanage or steal estate property. But a bond costs money, and bond companies are not charitable organizations. Assuming you've appointed someone trustworthy to be property guardian, there's no reason to be fearful about mismanagement, and so no reason to deplete your estate by the cost of a bond.

PROPERTY GUARDIANSHIPS AND CHILDREN'S TRUSTS

Although it's preferable to have property you leave your minor children managed in a children's trust, it's always advisable to name a property guardian as a backup. Why are trusts preferable to property guardianships? Property guardians typically must make frequent burdensome reports to a court, which usually means paying a lawyer to get the job done. In addition, state law often imposes restrictions and controls on how a property guardian can spend children's property. By contrast, a trustee of a children's trust is essentially free of court supervision and reporting requirements, and has broad power to use trust money for the child's living expenses, health needs and education. Finally, a property guardian must turn property over to the minor when he or she becomes a legal adult at age 18, while property left in a children's trust is turned over to the child at the age you specify (up to 35).

C. Other Concerns About Children

Here I look at some other issues that may arise concerning children.

1. Simultaneous Death and Minor Children

Parents of young children are often understandably concerned about what will happen to their children if both parents die simultaneously in an accident. Be assured that whatever choices you've made in your will should go into effect if both parents suddenly die, subject to court approval.

By making your will, you are doing your best to make sure that your children have a suitable personal adult guardian, and that any property of the children, including all property you leave them, is managed by an adult of your choice. Of course, to minimize confusion in the case of a simultaneous death, the wills of both spouses should be consistent with respect to these matters.

2. Adult Children

The word "children" has two meanings. The first is minors—people who are not legal adults, usually under age 18. The second meaning refers to offspring of any age. Parents obviously can have children who are themselves adults.

Parents of young adults may be reluctant to allow their children to receive outright significant amounts of property, simply because the children aren't mature enough to handle the property sensibly. In this situation, you can create a children's trust for your young adult children between ages 18 and 35, using the will forms in this book.

Example: *Carlotta and Ben, both in their late 50s, leave all their property to each other. Each names their two children, Ed and Charles, as equal alternate beneficiaries. Charles is 19 and Ed is 23. Their parents feel neither is yet mature enough to be prudent with money. So Carlotta and Ben both create a children's trust, with each child receiving his property outright when he reaches age 35. Carlotta and Ben both name Ben's sister, Marcella, as the trustee.*

Of course, you don't have to create a children's trust if you're leaving property to adult children, and often it's wiser not to. No one can really predict that a child will be more prudent financially at age 30 or 35 than at 20 or 25. Why possibly restrict the money your child may need—for a house, education or whatever—for a number of years? Many parents simply feel better to leave the money outright.

3. Disinheritance

To an outsider, it may seem sad that a parent would want to disinherit a child of any age, excluding that child from receiving any property from the parent's estate. Nevertheless, it's surely been known to happen. It's legal to disinherit a child as long as it is clear that the disinheritance is intentional, rather than accidental.

The wills in this book require you to list all your children. The wills further provide that: "If I do not leave property in this will to one or more of my children or grandchildren whom I have identified above, my failure to do so is intentional." Thus, if you do not leave any property to one of your children in your will, you have formally and legally disinherited that child. If you desire to be more explicit and include an express statement of disinheritance of a child as part of your will, you'll need another will resource. (See Chapter 11, Going Further, Section A.)

Normally, you don't have to list any grandchildren in your will. However, if a child dies leaving children, those grandchildren (of yours) legally stand in the place of the deceased child, so revise your will to list those grandchildren. (See Chapter 10, Changing or Revoking Your Will, Section A.) If you don't list those grandchildren in your will, they may have a right to inherit some of your property. If you don't leave property to grandchildren listed in your will, the will forms provide, as stated above, that your failure to leave them property was intentional.

If you have a child or adopt any children after your will is done, you should prepare a new will. In the new one, you list your new child's name, and leave him or her property (or don't) as you choose. (See Chapter 10, Changing or Revoking Your Will, Section A.) ■

Your Executor

Y our executor is the person you name in your will to assume legal responsibility for handling your property and distributing it as your will directs. Your executor's most important job is to carry out the terms of your will by transferring property to those to whom you left it. Under the wills in this book, your executor will also decide how your debts, probate fees and any estate taxes will be paid, following guidelines set by state law.

Your executor is also the person with legal authority to hire a lawyer for any probate proceedings. The reality of these proceedings is that the executor normally does little but sign papers, while wondering why the process is dragging on. Your executor is entitled to a fee for services, usually determined by a judge, which will be paid from your estate. The lawyer's fees, unsurprisingly, get paid from your estate as well.

Your executor's job ends once any probate proceeding is completed, which includes having distributed property as your will directed.

A. Choosing Your Executor

The most important criterion in naming your executor is to choose a responsible adult you trust completely. Many people name an executor who benefits substantially under the will, such as a spouse or adult child. This is fully legal and usually makes sense, as an executor who has a financial stake in how your property is distributed is likely to do a conscientious job. And since, by law, an executor is entitled to a fee for services, why not give this fee to a close family member or friend? Of course, there is a potential downside. If some inheritors don't trust or are jealous of the executor, there can be bickering or, even worse, serious conflict between family members. Ask yourself the following question: Who do you think would do the best job, be completely honest and aboveboard? Whether or not other family members agree with your choice, ultimately it's your decision.

Be sure to name someone who's willing to do the job. Obviously, you should discuss this ahead of time and receive his or her consent to serve before finalizing your decision. You will want to name someone who is healthy and likely to be around after your death.

You should always select at least one successor executor to serve if your executor cannot. Obviously, use the same criteria when choosing your successor executor as you did for your first choice.

Naming an out-of-state executor. Generally, you have unfettered freedom to name whomever you choose to be your executor. But some states' laws restrict the right of a nonresident to serve. Most of these laws merely require some additional paperwork. However, the following states impose more serious restrictions:

- *Kentucky* and *Florida*: nonresident may not serve unless legally related to will writer;

- *Tennessee* or *Wyoming*: nonresident must be legally related to will writer, or appointed to serve with another person who is a resident;

- *Ohio*: nonresident must be legally related to will writer, or a resident of a state that does not bar nonresidents from serving;

- *Nevada*: nonresident cannot serve as executor.

For many people, the choice of executor is obvious—their spouse, or mate. Others select a best friend or close family relation. If no one readily comes to mind as your executor, you have to work through your possible selections, using common sense to decide who would be the wisest choice. Do remember that human concerns are usually much more important than any technical expertise—an executor has the authority to hire experts if he or she needs them.

If you find there is no one at all you can rely on to be your executor, I urge you to keep trying to come up with someone who can serve. But if you really can't, you'll have to see if a financial institution, such as a bank or trust company, will accept the job. Unfortunately, financial institutions often don't work well as executors for modest to moderate estates. Banks and trust companies can be quite impersonal, as many beneficiaries have ruefully learned. Also, a modest estate is unlikely to be a high priority for a financial institution. Still, some people with modest estates end up with a financial institution as executor, because they just do not know any person they trust to do the job.

IF YOU WANT TO NAME CO-EXECUTORS

With a will from this book, you can only appoint one person to serve as your executor and another person to serve as successor executor. Appointing co-executors requires making decisions beyond the scope of this book, such as:

- Must all co-executors agree before any action can be taken?

- Must the agreement be in writing?

- Can any one executor act on behalf of the estate? And if so, under what restrictions?

Nevertheless, there are some situations where the will writer decides it's best—for reasons ranging from practicality to trying to maintain, or promote, family harmony—to name two or more people to serve as co-executors. If you want to do this, you'll need another resource. (See Chapter 11, Going Further, Section A.)

B. No Bond Required

A bond is a financial guarantee that your estate would be reimbursed should the executor mismanage or steal estate property. The wills in this book specify that no bond is required of an executor. Here's why: The cost for a bond would come out of your estate, and there is usually no sensible reason to have any of your property eaten up by a bond company. If you appoint a trustee you have complete faith in, there's simply no good purpose for a bond. But if you must select someone you don't know well, or don't fully trust, you may want a bond posted. If so, *do not* use a will form from this book. You'll need to see an attorney.

Unless you've stated in your will that your executor shall not be required to post a bond, many courts require one before approving a will. Occasionally, a court may require a bond to be posted by an out-of-state executor, no matter what you say in your will, but rarely does this actually occur. ∎

CHAPTER 6

Estate Planning

Estate planning means, for our purposes, arranging for the most efficient and economical transfer methods of your property upon your death. This chapter provides a summary overview of major aspects of estate planning so you can see if there are any areas you want to pursue. Also, you may need to understand some estate planning basics to sensibly prepare your will.

Most readers of this book should have no reason to pursue extensive estate planning, which requires time, thought and spending some money. If a basic will takes care of your needs, why do more? As discussed earlier, most estate planning is primarily a concern for older people who have accumulated a fair amount of property, or ill people of any age. (If, after reading this chapter, you decide to investigate estate planning in more depth, see Chapter 11, Going Further.)

A. What Is Probate?

If you die leaving a valid will, the property you've left by will is distributed following a court process called probate. I summarized the probate procedure in Chapter 1, How This Book Works, Section B. Here I'll note that some state laws permit a simplified probate process for small estates that is relatively quick and inexpensive. And a few states, including Texas and Wisconsin, have adopted streamlined probate laws that lessen lawyer involvement and reduce lawyers' probate fees substantially. But in most states, probate remains a hassle. The usual probate process often takes a year or more and runs up substantial lawyer fees, usually thousands of dollars.

The main advantage to probate is that it provides a short time period for a creditor to sue an estate. However, few estates—and certainly, very few moderate estates—face any serious creditor claims, so there isn't much of a benefit, if any, for most people.

Another possibly desirable aspect of probate is that a court supervises distribution of your property, which is sensible only if you don't trust your executor.

B. Avoiding Probate

Due to the drawbacks of probate, it's often sensible to arrange to have your property pass outside of probate, especially if death is likely to occur reasonably soon (like in the next decade or two). Thus, many older people prepare a thorough probate avoidance plan. By contrast, if you're young, you probably needn't bother to arrange to avoid probate now. After all, probate has no impact until you die. As I've already discussed in Chapter 1, most younger people are well-served by a basic will, and can sensibly postpone dealing with probate avoidance for quite a while.

The most common ways to pass property outside of probate are by use of the following:

- *Revocable living trust.* This is the most popular probate avoidance device. You create this legal entity by preparing and signing a trust document that specifies whom you want to receive your property at your death. A living trust essentially functions just like a will, except it avoids probate. Technically, you transfer whatever property you want to the trustee(s) of your living trust, which involves re-registering title of property in your name as trustee of your trust. But during your lifetime, you retain full control over your trust property—in other words, you can change or revoke a revocable living trust for any reason, and you can sell or buy any property from or for the trust. No trust income tax returns are required, and you don't have to maintain separate trust records. When you die, all trust property is transferred to your beneficiaries outside of probate.

- *Joint tenancy and tenancy by the entirety.* Each joint tenant owns equal shares of property, such as a house, securities or a bank account. In some states, joint tenancy property held by a married couple is called "tenancy by the entirety." When one joint tenant dies, his or her share automatically goes to the surviving joint tenant(s). If you attempt to use your will to leave your portion of joint tenancy property to someone other than the other joint tenant, you won't be successful. You cannot transfer joint tenancy property by will—with one exception: If both (or all) joint tenants die simultaneously, each joint tenant's share of the property passes under his or her will to the beneficiary of the residuary estate.

- *Life insurance.* Proceeds of a life insurance policy pass directly to the beneficiary or beneficiaries named on the policy. Only if you designate your own estate as the policy beneficiary (which is very rarely done, and not desirable for people using a basic will) are the proceeds subject to probate.

- *Pay-on-death bank accounts.* With pay-on-death accounts, you name on the account form a person (or persons) to receive any money remaining in your checking, savings or bank money market account or certificate of deposit at your death. While you're alive, you can withdraw money from the account or change the beneficiary. The beneficiary has no rights to any of the account funds until your death. These accounts are sometimes called "savings bank," "Totten trust" or "informal trust" accounts.

- *Transfer on death securities accounts.* The states listed below have adopted the Uniform Transfers-on-Death Securities Registration Act, which allows you to name a beneficiary, or beneficiaries, for any securities account (brokerage, stock and bonds account) or individual security where you actually hold the stock/bond certificate. This law works similarly to pay-on-death bank accounts. When you die, the beneficiary(ies) you've named for the securities account receive(s) it directly, outside of probate.

As of the date of the second edition of this book, the following states have adopted this law:

Alabama	Maryland	Oklahoma
Alaska	Minnesota	Oregon
Arizona	Mississippi	Pennsylvania
Arkansas	Missouri	South Dakota
Colorado	Montana	Tennessee
Connecticut	Nebraska	Texas
Delaware	Nevada	Utah
Florida	New Hampshire	Virginia
Idaho	New Jersey	Washington
Illinois	New Mexico	West Virginia
Iowa	North Dakota	Wisconsin
Kansas	Ohio	Wyoming

- *IRAs, profit-sharing and other retirement plans.* Many retirement plans—including IRAs, profit-sharing and 401(k) plans—allow you to name an adult beneficiary or beneficiaries to receive any funds remaining in the plan when you die. You can also arrange to leave these types of property to minors with an adult manager.

- *Gifts made during your lifetime.* Any property you give away while you are alive is not part of your estate when you die, so it is not subject to probate. Making a gift during life requires that you completely relinquish all ownership and control over the property to someone else.

C. Reducing Federal Estate Taxes

Federal estate taxes are assessed on net estates worth over a specific amount in the year of death. As mentioned in Chapter 1, the personal estate tax exemption allows a set dollar amount of property to pass tax-free, as shown below:

Year of Death	Amount of Personal Exemption
1998	$625,000
1999	$650,000
2000-2001	$675,000
2002-2003	$700,000
2004	$850,000
2005	$950,000
2006 and after	$1,000,000

Reminder: I use the term "estate tax threshold" to mean the amounts of the personal exemption in any and all years.

In addition to the amount of the personal exemption, all property one spouse leaves to the other is exempt from estate tax, no matter how much that property is worth.

Federal estate taxes are graduated and stiff. They begin at 37% for amounts between $650,000 and $750,000 and rise to 55% for amounts over $3,000,000. (While it may not be a consolation, U.S. death tax rates are lower than other Western countries.)

A majority of states have abolished death taxes, but some still have them. They're called "estate taxes" in some states and "inheritance taxes" in others. For our purposes, the technical differences between these two forms of state death taxes don't matter. Whatever the label, a state death tax means another bite from the estate. But even if you live in a state that has death taxes, they are rarely worth bothering about or planning to avoid, because the tax bite isn't that large (though it can sting).

If either your state alone, or the combined value of your own and your spouse's estate, exceeds the estate tax threshold, you may want to explore the possibility of planning to reduce your federal estate tax exposure. Why would a couple with a combined estate of, say, $1.3 million need to worry about estate tax? Assuming the couple owns their property equally, each one's share is $650,000, which is under the estate tax threshold no matter what year a spouse dies in. True, but usually spouses want to leave the bulk, or all, of their property to each other. Then the combined total of property may well exceed the estate tax threshold, and so be subject to a hefty estate tax when the surviving spouse dies. Estate tax planners call this "the second tax."

Example: *Maurice and Patricia have a combined estate of $900,000. Each leaves his or her estate of $450,000 to the other. Maurice dies in 1999. No federal estate taxes are due on his death, because his estate is under $650,000. Patricia's estate is now $900,000. She dies in 2002, leaving her property equally to their two children. $700,000 is exempt from tax. $200,000 is subject to federal tax. The tax assessed is $75,000, not a trivial amount. With good estate planning, this second tax could have been avoided and Maurice's property still left for Patricia's benefit while she lived.*

The main methods for achieving tax savings here are special estate tax-savings trusts and giving some of the property away while the original owner is alive.

A widely used trust for couples with a combined estate over the estate tax threshold is called an "AB" or "Marital Life Estate" trust. In these trusts, each spouse leaves property in trust for the other (surviving) spouse for that spouse's lifetime. After the surviving spouse dies, the trust property goes to whomever the first spouse named as final beneficiaries. The benefit of such a trust is that each spouse's property is kept separate for estate tax purposes, so the "second tax" is avoided.

There can be drawbacks to an AB trust. The deceased spouse's property is restricted by the terms of the trust; the surviving spouse doesn't have free use of that property. If a spouse may outlive the other by many years, the couple may not want property tied up for so long. (This just scratches the surface of AB trusts. If you want to explore this matter further, see Chapter 11, Going Further.)

D. Second Marriages

Members of couples in second/subsequent marriages who have children from a prior marriage often face a conflict: how to provide for their current spouse and also insure that the bulk of their property remains intact for their children to eventually inherit. A common solution is to use a type of life estate trust, sometimes called a "property control" trust, which divides use and control of trust property as the trust creator wants. These trusts need to be prepared by a lawyer.

Of course, in some second/subsequent marriages, couples agree on how their property should be distributed without bothering with a trust. For instance, both spouses may agree that 70% of either's property goes outright to the surviving spouse, with the remaining 30% going to the deceased spouse's child or children. In this situation, a trust won't be needed.

Although a trust isn't mandatory for estate planning in second/ subsequent marriages, you should make sure that both spouses, and preferably all children involved, understand and accept (whether enthusiastically or not) how the spouses' property will be distributed at death. If you think there's any realistic possibility of a conflict between any of the players, you really do need a lawyer.

E. Other Property Control Matters

There are other situations when people want to impose controls on their property and those who are to receive it. The usual solution is to create a trust imposing limits on how and when property may be used. For example, this may be the best way to provide for someone with a physical or mental disability. This is called a "special needs trust." You'll need help from a lawyer to prepare such a trust.

F. Durable Powers of Attorney

Part of estate planning includes arranging for who will handle your medical and financial affairs if you become incapacitated and are unable to do so. This is a grim concern, but at least there are simple, binding documents you can prepare to specify a person authorized to make decisions for you, or enforce decisions you've made. (If you want more information on either type of durable power of attorney described below, see Chapter 11, Going Further.)

1. Durable Power of Attorney for Health Care

With a durable power of attorney for health care, you can:

- appoint an adult to have legal authority to make health care decisions for you if you can't, and

- provide specific binding instructions for what must be done, or not done, in certain situations. A common concern is use of life support systems; many people specify that no artificial means be used to extend their lives, and that they be allowed to die a natural death.

This document can go by various names, such as a "health care directive." Also, in some states, you can also use a document called a "living will" (or similar wording) to accomplish one or both of these goals. A living will has nothing to do with a regular will, where you leave property. A living will is used only for health care matters.

2. Durable Power of Attorney for Financial Affairs

A durable power of attorney for financial affairs allows you to name someone with authority to handle all your money matters if you cannot. You can limit this person's authority as you see fit. For example, you can prohibit him or her from being able to sell your home within the restrictions you provide. The person you choose can legally handle all your financial affairs without any need for messy, costly court proceedings. ■

CHAPTER 7

Preparing the Draft of Your Will

This chapter explains how to prepare a draft of your will from one of the five forms in the Appendix. As you'll see, you'll fill in written information on the blank lines on a will form and cross out material that doesn't apply to your situation. When you've finished your draft, you'll need to have a final typed or word processed version of your will prepared.

Let's start with some encouraging words. For most people, the actual process of preparing a will is not very difficult. Certainly the process is comprehensible if you pay attention to the instructions. Don't feel intimidated; and go as slowly and carefully as is comfortable for you. Although preparing a will is a fairly straightforward process, it is obviously an important one that you will want to do right.

A. Determine Your Family Situation

The instructions in this chapter are designed to take you efficiently through the draft will writing process. There are different sets of instructions for different family situations. Which set of instructions should you use? Here's how to select the instructions and will form that are right for you.

- *If you are a parent.* Whether your children are minors or adults, turn to Section B if you are a parent. This includes adoptive parents who've legally adopted their children, but does not apply to stepparents.

- *If you don't have children but want to leave property of significant value to minors or young adults.* If you wish to leave property of significant value or money to other people's minor or young adult children, such as your nieces and nephews, turn to Section B.

- *If you don't have children.* If you don't have children and don't plan to leave anything of significant value to any minor or young adult children, turn to Section C.

Reminder: If you are getting divorced, but haven't obtained your final decree or order of divorce, you are still legally married for will writing purposes. Be sure to write a new will once the divorce is final.

B. How to Proceed If You Have Children (or Plan to Leave Property to Young People)

From the five different will forms in the Appendix, select the form that best describes your situation, as set out below:

- *A married person who wants his or her spouse to receive most property.* If you want to leave all or most of your property (except perhaps for a few specific gifts) to your spouse—or to your children if your spouse predeceases you—use Form 1. Instructions for Form 1 are below, in Section D.

- *A married person who wants to divide up property.* If you want to identify and distribute your property among several persons, including your spouse and children, you will want to use Form 5. But remember, any spouse still must leave at least 50% of his or her property to the spouse, or you must see a lawyer. Instructions for Form 5 are below, in Section E.

- *A member of an unmarried couple.* If you're a member of an unmarried couple with a child, or children, and you want a specific will clause to identify your mate, use Form 5. (This type of clause has no specific legal affect. It is a public acknowledgment of your relationship.) Otherwise, if you don't want a public statement about your relationship, use Form 3. Both sets of instructions are in Section E, below.

- *An aunt, uncle or other person who wants to leave property of significant value to minors.* Use Form 5, which allows you to set up a children's trust to manage property left to children who are under 35 when they inherit. Instructions for Form 5 are below, in Section E.

- *A single, divorced or widowed parent.* Use Form 3. Instructions are below, in Section E.

Each will form is located in the Appendix and is identified at the top of its first page by its number and a description, such as "Form 1. Married With Child(ren), Property to Spouse." To warn you about the obvious, if you tear out your will form, be sure you remove all pages of the form, and no pages from another will form. Each subsequent page of the will form is identified at the bottom of the page as "Form 1," "Form 3" and so on.

If you need additional forms (for instance, you and your spouse are both preparing wills or you just want extra copies of the form), photocopy your blank will form before filling in the draft.

C. How to Proceed If You're Not a Parent and Aren't Leaving Property of Significant Value to Young People

You'll find five different will forms in the Appendix. Start by selecting the form that best describes your situation, as set out below:

- *A married person.* Use Form 2. Instructions are below, in Section F.

- *A member of an unmarried couple.* If you want a specific will clause to identify your mate, use Form 4. (This type of clause has no specific legal effect. It is a public acknowledgment of your relationship.) Instructions for Form 4 are below, in Section F.

- *A single, divorced or widowed person.* Use Form 4. Instructions are below, in Section F.

Reminder: If you want to leave property of significant value to a minor child, turn to Section B, above and find the appropriate form.

Each will form is located in the Appendix and is identified at the top of its first page by its number and a description, such as "Form 2. Married With No Child(ren)." To warn you about the obvious, if you tear out your will form, be sure you remove all pages of the form, and no pages from another will form. Each subsequent page of the will form is identified at the bottom of the page as "Form 2," "Form 4" and so on.

If you need additional forms (for instance, you and your spouse are both preparing wills or you just want extra copies of the form), photocopy your blank will form before filling in the draft.

D. Instructions For a Married Person Using Form 1

As I've described, Form 1 is designed exclusively for a married person who wants to leave all of his or her property to a spouse, with the possible exception of a few minor gifts. The couple's children are named as alternate beneficiaries, who will receive the will writer's property if the spouse dies before the will writer. In other words, this will is "hard wired" to make it as easy as possible to prepare a will.

Don't change the basic will form you use! Making any changes to a basic will form other than simple commonsense ones, such as adjusting pronouns, is risky. The purpose of a basic will is to provide clarity and simplicity.

By making changes, you risk creating a confusing and possibly even ineffective document. If you want to make substantial changes to a will form, you need a more comprehensive will-drafting resource than this book provides. (See Chapter 11, Going Further, Section A, for a list of other Nolo will writing resources.)

The Top of the Will Form

Fill in your name in the first two blank lines at the top of the form. Use the name you customarily use when you sign legal documents and other important papers. If you've used different names—for instance, you changed your name to Jerry Adams, but still own some property in the name of Jerry Adananossos—identify yourself with both names: "Jerry Adams, aka Jerry Adananossos." ("Aka" stands for "also known as.")

In the next blank lines, fill in the county or township, followed by the state in which you live.

Will Section 1. *Revocation*

This standard language appears in all well-prepared wills. It revokes (invalidates) all previous wills, thus preventing possible confusion or litigation over the validity of any prior wills. A revocation clause is included in your will whether or not you actually have made an earlier will; you don't need to add or delete anything here.

Destroy old wills. Tear up or otherwise destroy the original and all copies of wills you made earlier. It is wisest not to rely solely on this revocation clause to make them invalid. The revocation clause is legal and enforceable, but someone with an earlier will might be inclined to challenge your current will. Certainly, there's nothing to be gained by leaving prior wills around.

Will Section 2. *Marital Status*

Form 1 states that you are married. In the blank line, fill in your spouse's name. Use the name he or she uses on official documents, such as a driver's license, tax returns or bank accounts.

WHAT HAPPENS IF SPOUSES DIE SIMULTANEOUSLY?

I mention simultaneous death again here because so many married couples are troubled by the possibility of it. As I explained earlier, the 45-day survivorship clause in the will controls what happens if a couple who left property to each other dies at or near the same time. Property left to the other spouse passes to the named alternate beneficiaries. The will form does not have a clause that explicitly addresses the simultaneous death of the will writer and spouse, because this is handled by the survivorship clause. (See Chapter 2, Your Beneficiaries, Section C.)

Will Section 3. *Children*

Will Form 1 states: "I have the following child(ren)." In the blank space, list each child's name and date of birth. Doing so shows that you didn't inadvertently overlook any of your children when making your will, which might otherwise automatically entitle them to a share of your estate. The will form provides that if you don't specifically leave property to a child named in your will, you made this decision intentionally.

Listing children on a will form involves naming all of your natural born and legally adopted children, and any children born while you were not married. Do not list stepchildren unless you have gone to court and legally adopted them. You cannot use your will to (try to) provide for children who may be born in the future. If you have a child after making your will, you need to revise your will (either by preparing a codicil to your existing will, or a new one).

Example: *I have the following children:*

Name	Date of Birth
Jack Goodman	9/8/55
Jennifer Goodman	12/14/60

Special rules for some grandchildren. Here's something that rarely applies to people writing basic wills, but if it does, you definitely need to handle it. In many states, if any of your children have died, their children have the same protection against being accidentally overlooked in your will as your own children. So if a child of yours has died and that child had children, list all of that child's children in your will. Also fill in the word "grandchild" in parentheses following each grandchild's name.

Example: *I have the following children:*

Name	Date of Birth
Beth Smith	7/1/67
Starr Smith	8/23/70
Melinda Smith	1/24/ 72
Benjamin Smith Myerson	5/7/90 (grandchild)

The will forms provide that if you haven't specifically left property to a grandchild listed in your will, you made that decision intentionally.

Will Section 4. *Specific Gifts*

To remind you, specific gifts are items of property you want to leave to a designated person or persons or an organization. (See Chapter 2, Your Beneficiaries, Section A.) Specific gifts can range from family mementos with no monetary value to a house, cash, car or other substantial asset.

As you know, Will Form 1 is designed solely for a married person who wants to leave all or most of his or her property to the other spouse, with the couple's child or children as alternate beneficiaries. The will achieves this by use of a residuary clause, which states that all property not otherwise given away by the will or other valid methods goes to the will writer's spouse, with the children as alternates.

This will provides two options for leaving gifts. The will writer can either:

- make up to three specific gifts and leave the bulk of his or her property to the spouse, or

- simply leave all of his or her property to the spouse, and make no specific gifts.

If you're not making any specific gifts, cross off the entire Will Section 4, and proceed to the instructions for Will Section 5. Later, you'll renumber the sections of your will before typing it.

Will Form 1 contains space for you to make only three specific gifts, because most people using this form won't want to make more than that. If, however, you want to make more, that's certainly okay. Simply remove the page marked "Additional Specific Gifts" from the Appendix, make any additional specific gifts on that form, and attach that page to your draft will form, with directions that it be inserted directly after the other specific gifts in Will Section 4, when your final version is prepared.

If you want to make one or more specific gifts, here's precisely how to do that. For each specific gift (or combination of gifts), identify the property in the first blank lines. In the next blank after the word "to," name the primary beneficiary or beneficiaries. Finally, name the alternate beneficiary(ies) in the last blank (assuming you're naming alternates). Repeat this process for each separate specific gift you make. If you've already prepared a beneficiary list, here's where you transfer that information to your will draft.

Example 1: *I leave* ___all my baseball cards___ *to* ___Theodore Zywansky___ *or, if such beneficiary does not survive me, to* ___Michael Smith___ .

Example 2: *I leave* ___my timeshare interest in the condominium apartment at 2 Park Avenue, Fort Lauderdale, Florida___ , *to* ___Elliott Russell and Noreen Russell___ , *or, if such beneficiaries do not survive me, to* ___Sheila Marks___ .

What's important for most will writers is that there are no rules that require property for separate gifts to be listed in any particular form or legal language. You need only identify the property with sufficient clarity so that there can be no question as to what you intended to give.

Most people using Form 1 should have no problems identifying property they leave as specific gifts. Their big-ticket items will be left to their spouse in the residuary estate. But if you are using Form 1 and want some assistance on how to describe property left as specific gifts, see Section E, instructions for Will Section 4, below.

The next portion of Will Section 4—after all the specific gifts, primary beneficiaries and alternate beneficiaries are listed—states that shared specific gifts are to be divided equally, unless specified otherwise. If you want to leave shared gifts to be divided unequally, review the instructions in Chapter 2, Your Beneficiaries, Section B. Further, the section provides that all shared gifts must be sold and the profits distributed as the will directs, unless all beneficiaries of that gift want to keep it, and agree to do so in writing.

Finally, this section explains that a deceased primary beneficiary's (or alternate beneficiary's) share of a shared gift will be shared equally by surviving beneficiaries (or alternate beneficiaries), unless otherwise specified. You don't do anything to this portion of Will Section 4.

Will Section 5. *Residuary Estate*

As you now know, your residuary estate consists of all property you don't leave by a specific will gift or that you have not left through other estate planning methods. Your residuary beneficiary receives all property in your residuary estate. With Form 1, all property in the residuary estate goes to your spouse. Your children are named as alternate residuary beneficiaries.

To complete this section, insert your spouse's name in the first blank. Then, in the next blank line, insert your child's or children's name(s) as your alternate beneficiaries. You can specify that each child takes an equal share, which the will form provides if you are silent on this matter, or you can specify a percentage of the total each child will receive if your spouse predeceases you.

Example: *I leave my residuary estate, that is, the rest of my property not otherwise specifically and validly disposed of by this will or in any other manner, to my spouse,*   Amanda Johnson   *, or, if my spouse does not survive me, to my children,* as follows: 30% to Derek Johnson ,   40% to Holly Johnson, and 30% to Brett Johnson   .

The next paragraph of Section 5 states that if there are two or more alternate residuary beneficiaries, all surviving alternate residuary beneficiaries evenly divide the portion of a deceased one. There are no other options with this will. You could, of course, attempt to create a third level of possible beneficiaries by naming successor alternate(s) for each alternate residuary beneficiary. However, attempting this leads to a will that is far more complicated than is needed by people this book is geared for. It's always possible to imagine endless levels of disaster. Indeed, it's part of lawyers' stock-in-trade to do so, ignoring the very low probabilities such disasters could occur. If you want more complexity or other options for handling alternate residuary beneficiaries, see a lawyer.

Finally, the last portion of this section defines "survive" to mean any beneficiary must outlive you by 45 days to inherit a gift you left.

Will Section 6. *Executor*

As you know from Chapter 5, Your Executor, this is the person you name in your will to have legal responsibility for handling your property after you die, and distributing it as your will directs.

Fill in the name of your executor in the first blank line. You should also name an alternate executor to serve if your first choice cannot, so fill in your alternate executor's name in the next blank line.

Example: *I name ___Gail Poquette___ as executor, to serve without bond. If that executor does not qualify, or ceases to serve, I name ___Maurice Poquette___ as executor, also to serve without bond.*

The final portion of Will Section 6 lists your executor's powers—the authority you give to your executor to manage your will estate. You don't need to add or change anything. The will authorizes broad powers that the executor may exercise at his or her discretion in carrying out the terms of your will. There's no reason to try to limit your executor's powers, as limitations could cause hassles when your executor attempts to wind up your estate. Since you've handpicked an executor you trust, there's no sensible reason to restrict that person's authority.

Will Section 7. *Personal Guardian*

If you have no minor children: Cross off this entire section and Will Section 8 and move on to Will Section 9.

Here you name the person responsible for raising your minor child or children, if you and the other parent cannot. Review the material in Chapter 4, Children, Section A, for guidelines on selecting a personal guardian.

Insert your choice for personal guardian on the first blank line of this will section. Name your alternate personal guardian on the second blank line.

Example: *If at my death any of my children are minors and a personal guardian is needed, I name   Steven Bronson   as the personal guardian, to serve without bond. If this person is unable or unwilling to serve as personal guardian, I name   Kathy Bronson-Brown   as personal guardian, also to serve without bond.*

Will Section 8. *Property Guardian*

Here you name your choices for your minor children's property guardian. (See Chapter 4, Children, Section B, for advice on selecting a property guardian.) Fill in the name of your choice for property guardian on the first blank line of this will section. Name your alternate property guardian on the second blank line.

Example: *If any of my children are minors and a property guardian is needed, I name   Steven Bronson   as the property guardian, to serve without bond. If this person is unable or unwilling to serve as property guardian, I name   Kathy Bronson-Brown   as property guardian, also to serve without bond.*

Will Section 9. *Children's Trust*

If you do not need, or want, to create a children's trust: Cross out this entire Will Section 9 and proceed to Chapter 8, Preparing Your Final Will.

As discussed in Chapter 4, Children, Section B, you may decide to use a children's trust for property you leave to your minor or young adult children. In this section, you fill in the blank lines to create a children's trust for each minor or young beneficiary you specify. You don't leave the property in this section. You've already done that when leaving specific gifts, or the residue.

It's important to recognize that your minor or young adult children could inherit significant amounts of property if your spouse (or other beneficiary) dies before you. Many will writers do leave significant amounts of property to their children as alternate beneficiaries, and so need to create a children's trust.

Of course, if your children don't stand to receive property of significant value under your will as primary, alternate or residuary (or alternate residuary) beneficiaries, you don't need to bother to establish a children's trust. What is property of "significant value?" Unfortunately, I can't give that term a set dollar figure. Life is too fluid for that. Remember, property left to be managed by the property guardian must be turned over to the child when he or she turns 18. One approach is to ask yourself, "If my child blows the inheritance at age 18 or 20, would that bother me?" If you're worried, it's a clear sign you want a children's trust for your minor/young adult children.

Will Subsection 9A. *Trust Beneficiaries and Age Limits*

To create a children's trust, fill in one minor/young adult beneficiary's name in the first blank line. Proceed down the blank lines below for any other trust beneficiaries, filling in a separate name in each line for as many trust beneficiaries as you want to name.

The will provides that each trust ends and each named beneficiary will receive his or her trust property outright when that trust's beneficiary becomes age 35, unless you have specified something different. If you want to choose a different age for any child to receive property, fill in that age in the blank line across from that child's name under the "Trust Shall End at Age" column. You can decide upon different ages for different children.

Example: *Each trust shall end when the following beneficiaries become 35 years of age, except as otherwise specified in this section.*

Trust Beneficiary	Trust Shall End at Age
Grady Watson	32
Daniel Watson	32
Shannon Watson	30

Will Subsection 9B. *Trustees*

Here you name the trustee of all children's trusts you have created in your will. You can only name one trustee and one successor (alternate) for all the children you've named as beneficiaries of a children's trust. (See Chapter 4, Children, Section B, for more on selecting a trustee.)

Insert the name of the trustee you've chosen on the first blank line. Insert the name of the successor trustee on the next blank line.

Example: *I name* _____Agnes Milgram_____ *as trustee, to serve without bond. If this person is unable or unwilling to serve as trustee, I name* _____Bobbie Robertson_____ *as successor trustee, also to serve without bond.*

Will Subsection 9C. *Beneficiary Provisions*

This clause gives your trustee considerable flexibility in spending trust money on or for your children. The trustee can spend trust money for the children's living needs and educational and medical expenses. The trustee determines what these needs are and how much to spend on them. The trustee must file separate income tax returns for each trust, but a court does not appoint or supervise the trustee. Do not add to or change this material.

Will Subsections 9D, 9E and 9F. *Termination of Trust, Powers of Trustee and Trust Administration Provisions*

The last three subsections of Section 9 of your will set out other terms of the children's trust. You don't add or change anything here. Subsection 9D provides that trust property will pass to the trust beneficiaries when they reach the age you specified, or age 35. If they die before reaching that age, the trust property will pass to their heirs.

Subsections E and F give the trustee broad discretionary powers to manage the trust property. The trustee may hire accountants, lawyers, investment advisors and other assistants. The trustee may also choose to be paid out of the trust property or income.

Congratulations! You have now completed your draft will. You're ready to proceed to Chapter 8, Preparing Your Final Will.

SIGNATURE CLAUSE

The signature clause comes at the end of your will, after the substantive sections, but before the witnesses clause. It does not have a section number. Don't sign or fill in any of these blank lines of your draft will or have it witnessed. This only happens with your final will, explained in the next chapter.

E. Instructions for Parents (or People Leaving Property to Children) Using Forms 3 or 5

If you have a child or children, or you're planning to leave property to minors or young adults, you'll use either:

- Form 3, if you are single, divorced or widowed, or

- Form 5, if you don't want to use Form 1 or 3. For example, you may be a member of an unmarried couple with children, a grandparent who wants to set up a children's trust or a married person who does not want to leave most or all of his property in bulk to the other spouse. (But remember, you still must leave at least 50% of your property to your spouse, or you'll need to see a lawyer.)

Now, you'll learn how to fill in a draft of either Form 3 or Form 5.

Don't change the basic will form you use! Making any changes to a basic will form other than simple commonsense ones, such as adjusting pronouns, is risky. The purpose of a basic will is to provide clarity and simplicity. By making changes, you risk creating a confusing and possibly even ineffective document. If you want to make substantial changes to a will form, you need a more comprehensive will-drafting resource than this book provides. (See Chapter 11, Going Further, Section A, for a list of other Nolo will writing resources.)

The Top of the Will Form

Fill in your name in the first two blank lines at the top of the form. Use the name you customarily use when you sign legal documents and other important papers. If you've used different names—for instance, you changed your name to Jerry Adams, but still own some property in the name of Jerry Adananossos—identify yourself with both names: "Jerry Adams, aka Jerry Adananossos." ("Aka" stands for "also known as.")

In the next blank lines, fill in the county or township, followed by the state in which you live.

Will Section 1. *Revocation*

This standard language appears in all well-prepared wills. It revokes (invalidates) all previous wills, thus preventing possible confusion or litigation over the validity of any prior wills. A revocation clause is included in your will whether or not you actually have made an earlier will; you don't need to add or delete anything here.

Destroy old wills. Tear up or otherwise destroy the original and all copies of wills you've made earlier. It is wisest not to rely solely on this revocation clause to make them invalid. The revocation clause is legal and enforceable, but someone with an earlier will might be inclined to challenge your current will. Certainly there's nothing to be gained by leaving prior wills around.

Will Section 2. *Marital Status*

Here you define your marital status. Whether you need to fill in anything depends on which form you use:

- Form 3 states: "I am not married." You don't need to add anything else here.

- Form 5 contains a blank line after the words "Marital Status." Fill in whatever fits your situation, among the following options:

"I am single."

"I am married to _____."

"My partner (or whatever term you use) is _____."

Use the name your spouse or partner uses on official documents, such as a driver's license, tax returns or bank accounts.

Will Section 3. *Children*

If you don't have any children or grandchildren: Cross off this entire section and move on to Will, Section 4. (You'll need to renumber that, and all subsequent, sections.) Will Forms 3 and 5 state: "I have the following child(ren)." In the blank space, list each child's name and date of birth. Doing so shows that you didn't inadvertently overlook any of your children when making your will, which might otherwise automatically entitle them to a share of your estate. The will form provides that if you don't specifically leave property to a child named in your will, you made this decision intentionally.

Listing children on a will form involves naming all of your natural born and legally adopted children, and any children born while you were not married. Do not list stepchildren unless you have gone to court and legally adopted them.

As previously discussed, if any of your children have died and that child had children, list each of those children in this Will section. Also, fill in the word "grandchild" in parentheses following each grandchild's name.

Example: *I have the following children:*

Name	*Date of Birth*
Astrid Valdez	*2/2/52*
Gene Valdez (grandson)	*4/7/79*
Celeste Valdez (granddaughter)	*6/18/84*

Will Section 4. *Specific Gifts*

To remind you, specific gifts are items of property you want to leave to a designated person or persons or an organization. (See Chapter 2, Your Beneficiaries, Section A.) Specific gifts can range from family mementos with no monetary value to a house, cash, car or other substantial asset.

Specific gifts are not required. If you want to leave all your property to one or a small group of beneficiaries in equal or unequal shares, you can cross out this entire section and skip to Will Section 5. But although specific gifts are certainly not required using any of the will forms, the majority of readers, based on my experience, will decide to make one or more.

Will Forms 3 and 5 contain space for you to make a few specific gifts, because most people won't want to make more than that. If, however, you want to make more, that's certainly okay. Simply remove the page marked "Additional Specific Gifts" from the Appendix, make any additional specific gifts on that form, and attach that page to your draft will form, with directions that it be inserted directly after the other specific gifts in Will Section 4, when your final version is prepared.

If you want to make one or more specific gifts, here's precisely how to do that. For each specific gift (or combination of gifts), identify the property in the first blank lines. In the next blank after the word "to," name the beneficiary or beneficiaries (whoever will be receiving the property) for that gift. Finally, name the alternate beneficiary(ies) in the last blank (assuming you're naming alternates). Repeat this process for each separate specific gift you make. If you've already prepared a beneficiary list, here's where you transfer that information to your will draft.

Example 1: *I leave* <u>all my baseball cards</u> *to* <u>Theodore Zywansky</u> *or, if such beneficiary does not survive me, to* <u>Michael Smith</u> .

Example 2: *I leave* <u>my timeshare interest in the condominium apartment at 2 Park Avenue, Fort Lauderdale, Florida</u> , *to* <u>Elliott Russell and Noreen Russell</u> , *or, if such beneficiaries do not survive me, to* <u>Sheila Marks</u> .

What's important for most will writers is that there are no rules that require your property be listed in any particular form or legal language. You need only identify the property with sufficient clarity so that there can be no question as to what you intended to give. Here are some tips that may help:

- *Real estate.* Identify a home or business by its street address: "my condominium at 123 45th Avenue, San Francisco, California" or "my summer home at 84 Memory Lane, Oakville, Missouri." For unimproved (empty) land, use the name by which it is commonly known: "my undeveloped 10-acre lot next to the McHenry Place on Old Farm Road, Sandusky, Ohio." Whatever the real estate, you don't need to list the legal description from the deed.

Real estate often includes items other than land and buildings. For instance, a farm may be given away with tools and animals, and a vacation home may be given away with household furnishings. If you intend to keep both together as one gift, state that in your specific gift—for example, "my cabin at the end of Fish Creek Road in Wilson, Wyoming, and all household furnishings and possessions in the cabin." If you want to separate household possessions from real estate, state that. For instance, "My condominium at 2324 Bayou Lane, Ft. Lauderdale, Florida, but not the possessions in that condominium." Then you could either leave your household possessions to named beneficiaries as you choose, or let them pass as part of your residuary estate.

- *Bank and other financial accounts.* List financial accounts as simply as possible. If you have only one account with a financial institution, you can simply list that institution's name and address. For instance, "my account at First Ames Bank, Ames, Iowa." Of course, you can list the account number too, which may make it easier to locate. If you have more than one account at the same institution, you must be more specific. For example: "Savings account #22222 at Independence Bank, Big Mountain, Idaho," "my money market account #2345 at Independence Bank, Big Mountain, Idaho."

- *Personal and household items.* You can separately identify and give away any items and possessions with great emotional or financial value—a photo album, an antique, a car or a work of art. If you own personal possessions that you don't want to bother itemizing, you can list them in categories: "all my tools," "all my dolls," "all my CD (compact disk) tapes, records, sheet music and piano." You can lump all your household possessions together: "all household furnishings and possessions in my house at 55 Drury Lane, Rochester, New York."

- *Shared gifts.* Name each person or organization who will receive a portion of the gift and then specify how it should be divided. You can leave the gift equally or you can divide ownership up in any way you decide. If you want the beneficiaries for a specific gift to receive unequal shares, indicate the percentage each beneficiary is to receive in parentheses after each of their names, making sure your numbers add up to 100%. If you don't specify a percentage, the will form provides that beneficiaries will share the property equally.

- *Multiple gifts to the same beneficiary(ies).* It is fine to give a number of items in one blank, as long as the items are all going to the same primary and alternate beneficiaries: "my Rolex watch, skis and coin collection" or "my dog, Gustav, my computer equipment and all my software."

Here are some other guidelines on naming beneficiaries:

- *Naming an individual.* List the full name by which the person is commonly known. This need not be the name that appears on a birth certificate, but it should clearly identify the person. Don't use terms such as "all my children," "my surviving children," "my lawful heirs" or "my issue." If you use broad or vague terms, it may lead to serious interpretation problems when you are not there to explain what you meant.

- *Naming organizations.* If you name a charity or a public or private organization, find out the organization's complete name. Several different organizations may use similar names—and you want to be sure your gift goes to the correct organization.

- *Pets.* As I discussed earlier, you cannot leave money directly to your pets in your will. However, you can leave money for their care to the person who has agreed to look after them in the event of your death.

- *Gifts to a couple.* If you want the gift to go to both members of a couple, list both of their names. If you want the gift to be shared equally between them, state that. If you want them to get unequal shares, indicate what percentage each member of the couple is to receive. If you list only one member of a couple, the gift will become that person's separate property.

- *Gifts to minors.* You can make specific gifts to minors either as primary beneficiaries or alternate beneficiaries. If you do either, you will probably want to complete the children's trust provision in Will Section 9.

The next portion of Will Section 4—after all the specific gifts, beneficiaries and alternates are listed—states that shared specific gifts are to be divided equally, unless specified otherwise. Further, the section provides that all shared gifts must be sold and the profits distributed as the will directs, unless all beneficiaries of that gift want to keep it, and agree to do so in writing.

Finally, this section explains that a deceased beneficiary's (or alternate beneficiary's) share of a shared gift will be shared equally by surviving beneficiaries (or alternate beneficiaries), unless otherwise specified. You don't do anything to this portion of Will Section 4.

Will Section 5. *Residuary Estate*

As you now know, your residuary estate consists of all property you don't leave by a specific gift or that you have not left through other estate planning methods. Your residuary beneficiary receives all property in your residuary estate.

With Will Forms 3 or 5, you name whoever you choose to take your residuary estate. Fill in that person's name, or people's names or an organization in the first blank lines of this section. You can, of course, name someone here whom you've also named as a primary or alternate beneficiary for a specific gift.

If you name more than one residuary beneficiary, decide whether you intend for them to share the residuary property equally. If so, you need only list their names—such as "Cynthia Kassouf, George Cobb and Bonita Cobb." Each will get a one-third share under the printed provision of the will. If you want them to take unequal shares, specify what percentage each should receive—such as "Cynthia Kassouf (50%), George Cobb (25%) and Bonita Cobb (25%)." And, of course, make sure that the percentages add up to 100%.

Next, you name your alternate residuary beneficiary (or beneficiaries). As I explained in Chapter 2, Your Beneficiaries, Section A, your alternate residuary beneficiary or beneficiaries are the last in line of your beneficiaries. He, she or they receive your property when other gifts fail because a primary beneficiary (and alternate) and residuary beneficiary are deceased. Realistically, this is unlikely to occur without there being time for you to prepare a new will reflecting your changed beneficiary situation. Still, naming an alternate residuary beneficiary provides one last backup against the state stepping in and directing who gets your property. Fill in the name or names of your alternate residuary beneficiary in the next blank line.

Example: *I leave my residuary estate, that is, the rest of my property not otherwise specifically and validly disposed of by this will or in any other manner, to* ____Lee Compton____ *or, if such residuary beneficiary does not survive me, to* ____Taylor Wright____ .

The next portion of Section 5 provides that any residuary gift made to two or more beneficiaries is shared equally among them unless you provide differently. This portion further states that a shared residuary gift must be sold, unless all the beneficiaries agree not to do so.

The next paragraph of Section 5 states that if there are two or more alternate residuary beneficiaries, all surviving alternate residuary beneficiaries evenly divide the portion of a deceased one. There are no other options with these wills. You cannot use wills from this book to assign unequal portions of a shared gift to different alternate residuary beneficiaries. In theory, you could attempt to create a third level of possible residuary beneficiaries, by naming successor alternate(s) for each alternate residuary beneficiary. Attempting this would lead to a will far more complicated than is needed by people this book is geared for. It's always possible to imagine endless levels of disaster. Indeed, it's part of lawyers' stock-in-trade to do so, ignoring the very low probabilities such disasters could occur. If you want more complexities or other options for handling alternate residuary beneficiaries, see a lawyer.

Finally, the last portion of this section defines "survive" to mean that any beneficiary must outlive you by 45 days to inherit a gift you left.

Will Section 6. Executor

As you know from Chapter 5, Your Executor, this is the person you name in your will to have legal responsibility for handling your property after you die, and distributing it as your will directs.

Fill in the name of your executor in the first blank line. You should also name an alternate executor to serve if your first choice cannot, so fill in your alternate executor's name in the next blank line.

Example: *I name* <u>Gail Poquette</u> *as executor, to serve without bond. If that executor does not qualify, or ceases to serve, I name* <u>Maurice Poquette</u> *as executor, also to serve without bond.*

The final portion of Will Section 6 lists your executor's powers—the authority you give to your executor to manage your will estate. You don't need to add or change anything. The will authorizes broad powers that the executor may exercise at his or her discretion in carrying out the terms of your will. There's no reason to try to limit your executor's powers, as limitations could cause hassles when your executor attempts to wind up your estate. Since you've handpicked an executor you trust, there's no sensible reason to restrict that person's authority.

Will Section 7. *Personal Guardian*

If you have no minor children: Cross off this entire section and Will Section 8 and move on to Will Section 9.

Here you name the person responsible for raising your minor child or children, if you and the other parent cannot. Review the material in Chapter 4, Children, Section A, for more on selecting a personal guardian.

Insert your choice for personal guardian on the first blank line of this will section. Name your alternate personal guardian on the second blank line.

Example: *If at my death any of my children are minors and a personal guardian is needed, I name* _____Steven Bronson_____ *as the personal guardian, to serve without bond. If this person is unable or unwilling to serve as personal guardian, I name* ____Kathy Bronson-Brown____ *as personal guardian, also to serve without bond.*

Will Section 8. Property Guardian

Here you name your choices for your minor children's property guardian. (See Chapter 4, Children, Section B, for advice on selecting a property guardian.) Fill in the name of your choice for property guardian on the first blank line of this will section. Name your alternate property guardian on the second blank line.

Example: *If any of my children are minors and a property guardian is needed, I name* _____Steven Bronson_____ *as the property guardian, to serve without bond. If this person is unable or unwilling to serve as property guardian, I name* _____Kathy Bronson-Brown_____ *as property guardian, also to serve without bond.*

Will Section 9. *Children's Trust*

If you do not need, or want, to create a children's trust: Cross out this entire Will Section 9 and proceed to Chapter 8, Preparing Your Final Will.

As discussed in Chapter 4, Children, Section B, you may decide to use a children's trust for property you leave to your minor or young adult children. You may also wish to leave property in trust to young people who aren't your children. In this section, you fill in the blank lines to create a children's trust for each minor or young beneficiary you specify.

You don't leave the property in this section. You've already done that when leaving specific gifts, or the residue.

Many will writers do leave significant amounts of property to their children or other young people as primary or alternate beneficiaries, and so need to create a children's trust. Of course, if your children and other young people don't stand to receive anything of significant value under your will as primary, alternate or residuary (or alternate residuary) beneficiaries, you don't need to bother to establish a children's trust. What is property of "significant value?" Unfortunately, I can't give that term a set dollar figure. Life is too fluid for that. One approach is to ask yourself, "If the beneficiary blows the inheritance at age 18 or 20, would that bother me?" If you're worried, it's a clear sign you want a children's trust for minor/young adult children.

Will Subsection 9A. *Trust Beneficiaries and Age Limits*

To create a children's trust, fill in one minor/young adult beneficiary's name in the first blank line. Proceed down the blank lines below for any other trust beneficiaries, filling in a separate name in each line for as many trust beneficiaries as you want to name.

The will provides that each named beneficiary will receive his or her trust property outright when that trust's beneficiary becomes age 35 unless you have specified something different. If you want to choose a different age for any beneficiary to receive property, fill in that age in the blank line across from his or her name under the "Trust Shall End at Age" column. You can decide upon different ages for different beneficiaries.

Example: *Each trust shall end when the following beneficiaries become 35 years of age, except as otherwise specified in this section.*

Trust Beneficiary	Trust Shall End at Age
Grady Watson	32
Daniel Watson	32
Shannon Watson	30

Will Subsection 9B. *Trustees*

Here you name the trustee of all children's trusts you have created in your will. You can only name one trustee and one successor (alternate) for everyone you've named as beneficiaries of a children's trust. (See Chapter 4, Children, Section B, for more on selecting a trustee.)

Insert the name of the trustee you've chosen on the first blank line. Insert the name of the successor trustee on the next blank line.

Example: *I name*   Agnes Milgram   *as trustee, to serve without bond. If this person is unable or unwilling to serve as trustee, I name*   Bobbie Robertson   *as successor trustee, also to serve without bond.*

Will Subsection 9C. *Beneficiary Provisions*

This clause gives your trustee considerable flexibility in spending trust money on or for the trust beneficiaries. The trustee can spend trust money for their living needs and educational and medical expenses. The trustee determines what these needs are and how much to spend on them. The trustee must file separate income tax returns for each trust, but a court does not appoint or supervise the trustee. Do not add to or change this material.

Will Subsections 9D, 9E and 9F. *Termination of Trust, Powers of Trustee and Trust Administration Provisions*

The last three subsections of Section 9 of your will set out other terms of the children's trust. You don't add or change anything here. Subsection 9D provides that trust property will pass to the trust beneficiaries when they reach the age you specified, or age 35. If they die before reaching that age, the trust property will pass to their heirs.

Subsections E and F give the trustee broad discretionary powers to manage the trust property. The trustee may hire accountants, lawyers, investment advisors and other assistants. The trustee may also choose to be paid out of the trust property or income.

Congratulations! You have now completed your draft will. You're ready to proceed to Chapter 8, Preparing Your Final Will.

SIGNATURE CLAUSE

The signature clause comes at the end of your will, after the substantive sections, but before the witnesses clause. It does not have a section number. Don't sign or fill in any of these blank lines of your draft will or have it witnessed. This only happens with your final will, explained in the next chapter.

F. Instructions for People Who Don't Have Children

If you don't have any children (and don't plan to leave significant property to minors), you'll use either:

- Will Form 2, if you're married, or

- Will Form 4, if you're single, divorced or widowed. Also, if you are a member of an unmarried couple without children, and you want to formally acknowledge your mate in your will, you can use Form 4 for that purpose.

Don't change the basic will form you use! Making any changes to a basic will form other than simple commonsense ones, such as adjusting pronouns, is risky. The purpose of a basic will is to provide clarity and simplicity. By making changes, you risk creating a confusing and possibly even ineffective document. If you want to make substantial changes to a will form, you need a more comprehensive will-drafting resource than this book provides. (See Chapter 11, Going Further, Section A, for a list of other Nolo will writing resources.)

The Top of the Will Form

Fill in your name in the first two blank lines at the top of the form. Use the name you customarily use when you sign legal documents and other important papers. If you've used different names—for instance, you changed your name to Jerry Adams, but still own some property in the name of Jerry Adananossos—identify yourself with both names: "Jerry Adams, aka Jerry Adananossos." ("Aka" stands for "also known as.")

In the next blank lines, fill in the county or township, followed by the state in which you live.

Will Section 1. *Revocation*

This standard language appears in all well-prepared wills. It revokes (invalidates) all previous wills, thus preventing possible confusion or litigation over the validity of any prior wills. A revocation clause is included in your will whether or not you actually have made an earlier will; you don't need to add or delete anything here.

Destroy old wills. Tear up or otherwise destroy the original, and all copies, of wills you made earlier. It is wisest not to rely solely on this revocation clause to make them invalid. The revocation clause is legal and enforceable, but someone with an earlier will might be inclined to challenge your current will. Certainly, there's nothing to be gained by leaving prior wills around.

Will Section 2. *Marital Status*

Here you define your marital status. How you do so depends on which form you use.

- Form 2 states: "I am married to _____." In the blank line, fill in your spouse's name.

- Form 4 states: "I am not married." You don't have to add anything here. If, however, you are a member of an unmarried couple, you may delete this sentence and replace it with, "My partner (or whatever term you use) is _____."

Will Section 3. *Specific Gifts*

To remind you, specific gifts are items of property you want to leave to a designated person or persons or an organization. (See Chapter 2, Your Beneficiaries, Section A.) Specific gifts can range from family mementos with no monetary value to a house, cash, car or other substantial asset.

Specific gifts are not required. If you want to leave all your property to one or a small group of beneficiaries in equal or unequal shares, you can cross out this entire section and skip to Will Section 4. But although specific gifts are certainly not required using any of the will forms, the majority of readers, based on my experience, will decide to make one or more.

Will Forms 2 and 4 contain space for you to make a few specific gifts, because most people won't want to make more than that. If, however, you want to make more, that's certainly okay. Simply remove the page marked "Additional Specific Gifts" from the Appendix, make any additional specific gifts on that form, and attach that page to your draft will form, with directions that it be inserted directly after the other specific gifts in Will Section 3, when your final version is prepared.

If you want to make one or more specific gifts, here's precisely how to do that. For each specific gift (or combination of gifts), identify the property in the first blank lines. In the next blank after the word "to," name the beneficiary or beneficiaries (whoever will be receiving the property) for that gift. Finally, name the alternate beneficiary(ies) in the last blank (assuming you're naming alternates). Repeat this process for each separate specific gift you make. If you've already prepared a beneficiary list, here's where you transfer that information to your will draft.

Example 1: *I leave* __all my baseball cards__ *to* __Theodore Zywansky__ *or, if such beneficiary does not survive me, to* __Michael Smith__ .

Example 2: *I leave* __my timeshare interest in the condominium apartment at 2 Park Avenue, Fort Lauderdale, Florida__ *, to* __Elliott Russell and Noreen Russell__ *, or, if such beneficiaries do not survive me, to* __Sheila Marks__ .

What's important for most will writers is that there are no rules that require your property be listed in any particular form or legal language. You need only identify the property with sufficient clarity so that there can be no question as to what you intended to give. Here are some tips that may help:

- *Real estate.* Identify a home or business by its street address: "my condominium at 123 45th Avenue, San Francisco, California" or "my summer home at 84 Memory Lane, Oakville, Missouri." For unimproved (empty) land, use the name by which it is commonly known: "my undeveloped 10-acre lot next to the McHenry Place on Old Farm Road, Sandusky, Ohio." Whatever the real estate, you don't need to list the legal description from the deed.

Real estate often includes items other than land and buildings. For instance, a farm may be given away with tools and animals, and a vacation home may be given away with household furnishings. If you intend to keep both together as one gift, state that in your specific gift—for example, "my cabin at the end of Fish Creek Road in Wilson, Wyoming, and all household furnishings and possessions in the cabin." If you want to separate household possessions from real estate, state that. For instance, "My condominium at 2324 Bayou Lane, Ft. Lauderdale, Florida, but not the possessions in that condominium." Then you could either leave your household possessions to named beneficiaries as you choose, or let them pass as part of your residuary estate.

- *Bank and other financial accounts.* List financial accounts as simply as possible. If you have only one account with a financial institution, you can simply list that institution's name and address. For instance, "my account at First Ames Bank, Ames, Iowa." Of course, you can list the account number too, which may make it easier to locate. If you have more than one account at the same institution, you must be more specific. For example: "Savings account #22222 at Independence Bank, Big Mountain, Idaho," "my money market account #2345 at Independence Bank, Big Mountain, Idaho."

- *Personal and household items.* You can separately identify and give away any items and possessions with great emotional or financial value—a photo album, an antique, a car or a work of art. If you own personal possessions that you don't want to bother itemizing, you can list them in categories: "all my tools," "all my dolls," "all my CD (compact disk) tapes, records, sheet music and piano." You can lump all your household possessions together: "all household furnishings and possessions in my house at 55 Drury Lane, Rochester, New York."

- *Shared gifts.* Name each person or organization who will receive a portion of the gift and then specify how it should be divided. You can leave the gift equally or you can divide ownership up in any way you decide. If you want the beneficiaries for a specific gift to receive unequal shares, indicate the percentage each beneficiary is to receive in parentheses after each of their names, making sure your numbers add up to 100%. If you don't specify a percentage, the will form provides that beneficiaries will share the property equally.

- *Multiple gifts to the same beneficiary(ies).* It is fine to give a number of items in one blank, as long as the items are all going to the same primary and alternate beneficiaries: "my Rolex watch, skis and coin collection" or "my dog, Gustav, my computer equipment and all my software."

Here are some other guidelines on naming beneficiaries.

- *Naming an individual.* List the full name by which the person is commonly known. This need not be the name that appears on a birth certificate, but it should clearly identify the person. Don't use terms such as "all my children," "my surviving children," "my lawful heirs" or "my issue." If you use broad or vague terms, it may lead to serious interpretation problems when you are not there to explain what you meant.

- *Naming organizations.* If you name a charity or a public or private organization, find out the organization's complete name. Several different organizations may use similar names—and you want to be sure your gift goes to the correct organization.

- *Pets.* As I discussed earlier, you cannot leave money either directly or in a trust for your pets. However, you can leave money for their care to the person who has agreed to look after them in the event of your death.

- *Gifts to a couple.* If you want the gift to go to both members of a couple, list both of their names. If you want the gift to be shared equally between them, state that. If you want them to get unequal shares, indicate what percentage each member of the couple is to receive. If you list only one member of a couple, the gift will become that person's separate property.

- *Gifts to minors.* These will forms do not have provisions for creating a children's trust. If you want to leave a gift to a minor, you can leave the gift directly to that child, with the property to be managed by a parent or parents or you can leave the gift to the parent(s) to use for the child. If you want to create a children's trust, you'll need to use Form 5 and follow the instructions in Section E, above.

The last portion of Will Section 3—after all the specific gifts, beneficiaries and alternates are listed—states that shared specific gifts are to be divided equally, unless specified otherwise. Further, the section provides that all shared gifts must be sold and the profits distributed as the will directs, unless all beneficiaries of that gift want to keep it, and agree to do so in writing.

Finally, this section explains that a deceased beneficiary's (or alternate beneficiary's) share of a shared gift will be shared equally by surviving beneficiaries (or alternate beneficiaries), unless otherwise specified. You don't do anything to this portion of Will Section 3.

Will Section 4. *Residuary Estate*

As you now know, your residuary estate consists of all property you don't leave by a specific gift or that you have not left through other estate planning methods. Your residuary beneficiary receives all property in your residuary estate.

With Will Forms 2 or 4, you name whoever you choose to take your residuary estate. Fill in that person's name or people's names or organization in the first blank lines of this section. You can, of course, name someone here whom you've also named as a primary or alternate beneficiary for a specific gift.

If you name more than one residuary beneficiary, decide whether you intend for them to share the residuary property equally. If so, you need only list their names—such as "Cynthia Kassouf, George Cobb and Bonita Cobb." Each will get a one-third share under the printed provision of the will. If you want them to take unequal shares, specify what percentage each should receive—such as "Cynthia Kassouf (50%), George Cobb (25%) and Bonita Cobb (25%)." And, of course, make sure that the percentages add up to 100%.

Next you name your alternate residuary beneficiary (or beneficiaries). As I explained in Chapter 2, Your Beneficiaries, Section A, your alternate residuary beneficiary or beneficiaries are the last in line of your beneficiaries. He, she or they receive your property when other gifts fail because a primary beneficiary (and alternate) and residuary beneficiary are deceased. Realistically, this is unlikely to occur without there being time for you to prepare a new will reflecting your changed beneficiary situation. Still, naming an alternate residuary beneficiary provides one last backup against the state stepping in and directing who gets your property. Fill in the name or names of your alternate residuary beneficiary in the next blank line.

Example: *I leave my residuary estate, that is, the rest of my property not otherwise specifically and validly disposed of by this will or in any other manner, to* _____Joanna Driscoll_____ *or, if such residuary beneficiary does not survive me, to* _____Bela Bergstrom_____.

The next portion of Section 4 provides that any residuary gift made to two or more beneficiaries is shared equally among them unless you provide differently. This portion further states that a shared residuary gift must be sold, unless all the beneficiaries agree not to do so.

The next paragraph of Section 4 states that if there are two or more alternate residuary beneficiaries, all surviving alternate residuary beneficiaries evenly divide the portion of a deceased one. There are no other options with these wills. You cannot use a will from this book to assign unequal portions of a shared gift to alternate residuary beneficiaries. In theory, you could attempt to create a third level of possible residuary beneficiaries, by naming a successor alternate for each alternate residuary beneficiary. Attempting this would lead to a will far more complicated than is needed by people this book is geared for. It's always possible to imagine endless levels of disaster. Indeed, it's part of lawyers' stock-in-trade to do so, ignoring the very low probabilities such disasters could occur. If you want more complexity or other options for handling alternate residuary beneficiaries, see a lawyer.

Finally, the last portion of this section defines "survive" to mean any beneficiary must outlive you by 45 days to inherit a gift you left.

Will Section 5. *Executor*

As you know from Chapter 5, Your Executor, this is the person you name in your will to have legal responsibility for handling your property after you die, and distributing it as your will directs.

Fill in the name of your executor in the first blank line. You should also name an alternate executor to serve if your first choice cannot, so fill in your alternate executor's name in the next blank line.

Example: *I name* <u>Gail Poquette</u> *as executor, to serve without bond. If that executor does not qualify, or ceases to serve, I name* <u>Maurice Poquette</u> *as executor, also to serve without bond.*

The final portion of Will Section 5 lists your executor's powers—the authority you give to your executor to manage your will estate. You don't need to add or change anything. The will authorizes broad powers that the executor may exercise at his or her discretion in carrying out the terms of your will. There's no reason to try to limit your executor's powers, as limitations could cause hassles when your executor attempts to wind up your estate. Since you've handpicked an executor you trust, there's no sensible reason to restrict that person's authority.

Congratulations! You have now completed your draft will. You're ready to proceed to Chapter 8, Preparing Your Final Will.

SIGNATURE CLAUSE

The signature clause comes at the end of your will, after the substantive sections, but before the witnesses clause. It does not have a section number. Don't sign or fill in any of these blank lines of your draft will or have it witnessed. This only happens with your final will, explained in the next chapter. ■

Preparing Your Final Will

O nce you've prepared a draft of your will following the instructions in Chapter 7, you're ready to finish the will-creating job and put your will into a legally correct form.

A. Getting Your Draft Ready for Typing

The first step is getting your will draft cleaned up for final typing. To do this, you need to make sure that all pages are in the correct order and that no extraneous material is typed on the final version of your will form. This can mean:

- *correcting any pronouns or other words in the form to precisely fit your will.* For instance, the alternate beneficiary clause in all the forms reads, "...if such beneficiary(ies) do(es) not survive me...." This should be corrected either to "...if such beneficiary does not..." or "if such beneficiaries do not...."

- *renumbering sections of your will.* In preparing your draft will, there may be sections in the form you use that you don't need. For example, if you decided not to make any specific gifts, you crossed out that section of your will. But once you've done so, the numbering of all subsequent sections of your will is off. You'll need to renumber all the following sections of your will so there are no gaps in the numbering.

- *deleting the blank lines.* If you prepare the final word processed or typed version of your will yourself, just be sure you omit the blank lines. But if you're having someone else prepare your will, you need to cross out the lines on your draft will. Just draw a pencil line through the printed underlines.

- *crossing out the title.* The large title at the top of your will form, and the will form indications on the bottom of subsequent pages (for example, "Form 4"), should not be typed in.

- *making sure all pages are in order.* If you added any extra "Specific Gifts" pages, make sure the page(s) follow(s) directly after the other printed specific gifts in your will.

When you review the will form, you'll notice that the witness clauses have printed material below the blank lines, specifying that the information written above is the will signer or a witness's name or a witness's address. It's fine to leave this identifying printed material on the form, to be included in your final will. Because witnesses' handwriting may not be picture perfect, having the identifying printed material below a witness's writing can be an aid later on. Certainly, having this printed material does no harm.

Next, make sure your will does what you want, and there aren't any mistakes. For most readers, the review process should be simple. If your situation is clear and you've followed the instructions in Chapter 7 carefully, your will is okay. But do be sure to check your draft will over thoroughly before moving on to having your final will prepared. It's well worth spending a little time to be absolutely sure your will says exactly what you want it to.

Now we'll focus on the requirements necessary to make your will legal. Fortunately, the formalities are easy. All you need to do is:

- make sure your will is neatly word processed (or typed), and

- sign it in front of two or three witnesses and have them sign it as well.

Below I examine both of these formalities in detail. If your will doesn't comply with these technical requirements—say it was typed but not witnessed—the will cannot be validated by the probate court, and your property will most likely pass as if no will existed. It's not hard to prepare a will correctly. But it's essential to check and double check to be sure you do.

B. Word Process or Type Your Will

The final will you prepare from this book must be completely word processed or typewritten. You can either prepare your final will from your draft yourself or have someone else do it. As long as it prints clearly, you can use an old portable typewriter, a laser printer or anything in-between.

Do not use a typewriter or handwriting to fill in the blanks of a will form in this book and try to use that as your final will. There are a number of reasons why doing this would be a bad idea. Most importantly, you'll have crossed out some material on the form, which would make it unusual, and thus perhaps suspect, to a probate judge. A will is not a place to explore unconventionality.

Finally, the wills in this book were not designed to be filled in. The paper dimensions of this book's will forms are not those conventionally used for wills.

Your will should be typed on regular 8-1/2" x 11" white bond paper. Paper with a high rag content looks nicer, but cheap paper is just as legal. Do not use erasable typing paper.

I recommend double spacing, although single spacing is permissible. Spacing should be uniform throughout the will. Use standard side and top margins; one inch on all sides is recommended. Number pages sequentially, preferably at the bottom of each page.

If your final will is prepared on a word processor, any mistakes or typos can be simply corrected, and the form reprinted before you sign it.

Typing mistakes can be machine-corrected, but there can be no handwritten corrections or cross-outs. If you "X" out or type over a mistake, you may inadvertently invalidate your will. Allowable machine corrections include use of self-correcting typewriters, and careful use of white-out, or correcting tape, and then retyping. However, don't do this extensively. If there are more than a few minor changes, retype your will.

If you are having someone else word process or type your final will, be sure that person:

- receives a neatly prepared draft so he or she won't make a mistake as a result of being confused

- understands exactly where any insertions are to be made in the will, and

- knows that the blank lines printed on the form, as well as any clauses you've drawn lines through, aren't to be typed or printed in the final will.

Commonsense Note: Your primary mission when you (or anyone else) types your will is to avoid any suspicion that you or anyone else changed your will after you engaged in the formal signing and witnessing. Accordingly, if a mistake is made on a sensitive item, say a beneficiary's name, you should retype the whole page rather than using typewriter correcting fluid or something similar. You don't want to create the possibility that a would-be beneficiary, or the probate judge, will question whether the change was valid.

C. Signing and Witnessing Your Will

To properly sign your will, you must first select a minimum of two witnesses. Three witnesses must see you sign your will if you live in Vermont. While only two witnesses are required in all other states, it's wisest to use three, if possible. If for some reason a witness has to be located after you die, there are better odds of finding one if you started with three, rather than two.

Your witnesses watch you sign your will, and then sign their names below your signature. You must do this correctly. Unless your will is properly witnessed, it won't be valid. Happily, it's easy to do it right. Notarization is not required to make a will legal. You won't use a notary unless you make your will "self-proving," as explained in Section D, below.

1. Selecting Qualified Witnesses

In most states, you can usually eliminate any need for your witnesses to appear in probate court if you also complete a self-proving affidavit. This requires use of a notary. See Section D, below. Otherwise, after your death, at least one of your witnesses may need to testify in court or swear through an affidavit that the document offered to probate is actually your will and that you were of sound mind when you made it.

Follow these guidelines when selecting your witnesses:

- If practicable, select three witnesses, even if only two are required.
- Choose people who are mentally competent and over age 18.
- Do not select a beneficiary of your will as a witness. This is important; if you leave property to a witness, that person may be disqualified as a witness or even disqualified from inheriting that property.
- Do not select your spouse or any of your children as witnesses.

2. Sign Your Will in the Presence of Your Witnesses

When you're ready to sign your will, call your witnesses together in one place. They need not read your will and you need not read it to them. However, they must all be aware that you intend the document to be your will. Explain to them that you want them to witness your will and identify the document before them as your will. There's no requirement that your explanation be laden with legalese. You could simply hold up your will and say, "Well, this is my will and I want you to witness it."

You must date the will and sign it in the presence of your witnesses. In the blanks provided, fill in the day, month and year you are signing the will as well as the county or township and state where you are signing it. Then sign in ink in the same form of your name you used in your will. For example, if you start your will with the name of Elissa T. James, sign your will the same way, not in another form, such as "E. T. James" or "Elissa Thelma James."

Once you've signed your will, ask your witnesses to date and sign it in ink with their normal signatures and fill in their addresses in the spaces indicated.

D. Self-Proving Affidavits

A self-proving affidavit is a simple document attached to your will where a notary public attests to your witnesses' signatures. Basically, the notary public signs and stamps his or her seal to a document attesting that your will was properly executed. Self-proving your will doesn't affect its validity—it simply eliminates the requirement that a witness appear in person or file a written affidavit at the probate proceeding after your death.

The advantage of a self-proving affidavit is that you've eliminated any possibility that your witnesses will have to go to court to testify that your will is valid. Since you hope your will won't go into effect for many years or many decades, it might be a little difficult, and sometimes impossible, to find a witness after so much time has elapsed.

The drawback to a self-proving affidavit it that you have to locate a notary. Usually, this isn't hard. Many banks or real estate offices (title companies) provide notary services. Then you have to get your witnesses to appear before the notary—a bit more of a hassle. Or perhaps you can ask the notary if there are folks in his or her office who can be witnesses. Your witnesses don't have to be friends of yours. They can be strangers to whom you show an ID in order to establish your identity. This occurs all the time in wills witnessed in law offices.

Even if you don't use a self-proving affidavit, your witnesses are unlikely to have to make a court appearance. There's now a strong national trend among the states to allow witnesses to a will to declare in an affidavit prepared after a will writer's death that they in fact witnessed the will (as opposed to actually appearing and testifying to this in court). Accordingly, including a self-proving affidavit with your will may not be the only way you can free your witnesses from the necessity of appearing in court. But if none of your witnesses can be located at all, and anyone questions the validity of your will (or, much less likely, a judge insists on a witness statement for an uncontested will), your estate may be in trouble unless you used a self-proving affidavit when you signed your will.

If you choose not to use a self-proving affidavit, move on to Section E.

States where you cannot use a self-proving affidavit from this book: You cannot use the self-proving affidavits provided in this book if you live in:

- *California, Michigan or Wisconsin.* Residents of these three states don't need to prepare self-proving affidavits; the declaration contained in the will form that witnesses sign makes the will self-proving.
- *District of Columbia, Maryland and New Hampshire.* New Hampshire allows self-proving of wills, but requires that special language be included as part of the will document, rather than on a separate form.
- *Ohio or Vermont.*

In states where you can use a self-proving affidavit, here's how to make your will self-proving:

Step 1. Locate a notary. Ask if the notary has a form for making your will self-proving. If so, you'll use that form, as the notary instructs, or

Step 2. If the notary does not have a form, select the correct form from the three different forms provided in the Appendix. You'll need to retype this form into an 8-1/2" by 11" format.

WHICH AFFIDAVIT TO USE

Use Form:	If you live in:
Affidavit-1	Alabama, Alaska, Arizona, Arkansas, Colorado, Connecticut, Hawaii, Idaho, Illinois, Indiana, Maine, Minnesota, Mississippi, Montana, Nebraska, Nevada, New Mexico, New York, North Dakota, Oregon, South Carolina, South Dakota, Tennessee, Utah, Washington or West Virginia.
Affidavit-2	Delaware, Florida, Georgia, Iowa, Kansas, Kentucky, Massachusetts, Missouri, New Jersey, North Carolina, Oklahoma, Pennsylvania, Rhode Island, Virginia or Wyoming.
Affidavit-3	Texas

Step 3. Sign your will and have it witnessed.

Step 4. Either have the notary present at the will signing or go to the notary at a later time. Either way, you and your witnesses must personally appear together before the notary.

IF THE NOTARY BALKS

Many notaries are familiar with self-proving affidavits, and will notarize your document without difficulty. However, some notaries are hesitant about notarizing this document because they correctly understand that they cannot properly notarize a will. If you encounter this problem, gently educate the notary, pointing out that you are not asking him or her to notarize your will, but a self-proving affidavit for the will, a document the notary can notarize.

Step 5. Write your name and your witnesses' names and addresses in the spaces indicated in the affidavit and give the form to the notary. The notary will have you and your witnesses swear to the truth of the statement in the affidavit. The notary will require some identification from you and your witnesses, such as a driver's license, before signing and dating the affidavit and putting the notary seal on it.

Step 6. Staple the affidavit to your will. If you ever make a new will, you must also make a new self-proving affidavit.

Reminder: The affidavit and will are two separate documents. Both you and your witnesses must sign your will in addition to signing this affidavit.

E. Sample Completed Will, Including Self-Proving Affidavit

Here is a sample completed will (by a will writer who lives in New Jersey and used Form 5), after it has been typed, signed and witnessed. This will also contains a signed, witnessed and notarized self-proving affidavit.

WILL OF DAVID WARFMAN

I, David Warfman, a resident of Essex County, State of New Jersey, declare that this is my will.

1. Revocation. I revoke all wills that I have previously made.

2. Marital Status. I am married to Melinda Wood Warfman.

3. Children. I have the following child(ren):

Name	Date of Birth
Jeremiah Warfman	6/20/85
Jasmine Warfman	1/2/87

If I do not leave property to one or more of the children or grandchildren whom I have identified above, my failure to do so is intentional.

4. Specific Gifts. I make the following specific gifts of property:

I leave my woodworking tools to my brother, Sidney Warfman or, if such beneficiary does not survive me, to his son, Phil Warfman.

I leave $10,000 to James Smith, with great appreciation for his skill in gardening or, if such beneficiary does not survive me, to Melinda Wood Warfman.

Any specific gift made in this will to two or more beneficiaries shall be shared equally among them, unless unequal shares are specifically indicated. All shared gifts must be sold, and the net proceeds distributed as the will directs, unless all beneficiaries for that gift agree in writing, after the will writer's death, that the gift need not be sold.

If I name two or more primary beneficiaries to receive a specific gift of property and any of them do not survive me, all surviving primary beneficiaries shall equally divide the deceased primary beneficiary's share unless I have specifically provided otherwise. If I name two or more alternate beneficiaries to receive a specific gift of property and any of them do not survive me, all surviving alternate beneficiaries shall equally divide the deceased alternate beneficiary's share.

5. Residuary Estate. I leave my residuary estate, that is, the rest of my property not otherwise specifically and validly disposed of by this will or in any other manner, to: 60% to my wife Melinda Wood Warfman, 20% each to Jeremiah Warfman and Jasmine Warfman or, if any residuary beneficiary does not survive me, to the survivors.

Any residuary gift made in this will to two or more beneficiaries shall be shared equally among them, unless unequal shares are specifically indicated. All shared residuary gifts must be sold, and the net proceeds distributed as the will directs, unless all beneficiaries for that gift agree in writing, after the will writer's death, that the gift need not be sold.

If I name two or more alternate residuary beneficiaries to receive property and any of them do not survive me, all surviving alternate residuary beneficiaries shall equally divide the deceased alternate residuary beneficiary's share.

As used in any section of this will, the word "survive" means to outlive the will writer by at least 45 days.

6. Executor. I name Melinda Wood Warfman as executor, to serve without bond. If that executor does not qualify, or ceases to serve, I name Sidney Warfman as executor, also to serve without bond.

I direct that my executor take all actions legally permissible to probate this will, including filing a petition in the appropriate court for the independent administration of my estate.

I grant to my executor the following powers, to be exercised as the executor deems to be in the best interests of my estate:

(1) To retain property, without liability for loss or depreciation resulting from such retention.

(2) To sell, lease or exchange property and to receive or administer the proceeds as a part of my estate.

(3) To vote stock, convert bonds, notes, stocks or other securities belonging to my estate into other securities, and to exercise all other rights and privileges of a person owning similar property.

(4) To deal with and settle claims in favor of or against my estate.

(5) To continue, maintain, operate or participate in any business which is a part of my estate, and to incorporate, dissolve or otherwise change the form of organization of the business.

(6) To pay all debts and taxes that may be assessed against my estate, as provided under state law.

(7) To do all other acts, which in the executor's judgment may be necessary or appropriate for the proper and advantageous management, investment and distribution of my estate.

These powers, authority and discretion are in addition to the powers, authority and discretion vested in an executor by operation of law, and may be exercised as often as deemed necessary, without approval by any court in any jurisdiction.

7. Personal Guardian. If at my death any of my children are minors and a personal guardian is needed, I name Esther Warfman as the personal guardian, to serve without bond. If this person is unable or unwilling to serve as personal guardian, I name Sidney Warfman as personal guardian, also to serve without bond.

8. Property Guardian. If any of my children are minors and a property guardian is needed, I name Melinda Wood Warfman as the property guardian, to serve without bond. If this person is unable or unwilling to serve as property guardian, I name Esther Warfman as property guardian, also to serve without bond.

9. Children's Trust. All property I leave in this will to any of the beneficiaries listed in Section A, below, shall be held for each of them in a separate trust, administered according to the following terms:

A. Trust Beneficiaries and Age Limits

Each trust shall end when the following beneficiaries become 35 years of age, except as otherwise specified in this section.

Trust Beneficiary	Trust Shall End At Age
Jeremiah Warfman	32
Jasmine Warfman	32

B. Trustees

I name Melinda Wood Warfman as trustee, to serve without bond. If this person is unable or unwilling to serve as trustee, I name Esther Warfman as successor trustee, also to serve without bond.

C. Beneficiary Provisions

(1) The trustee may distribute for the benefit of each beneficiary as much of the net income or principal of the trust as the trustee deems necessary for the beneficiary's health, support, maintenance and education. In deciding whether to make a distribution for or to a beneficiary, the trustee may take into account the beneficiary's other income, resources and sources of support.

(2) Any trust income that is not distributed to a beneficiary by the trustee shall be accumulated and added to the principal of the trust administered for that beneficiary.

D. Termination of Trust

The trust shall terminate when any of the following occurs:

(1) The beneficiary becomes the age specified in Paragraph A of this trust;

(2) The beneficiary dies before becoming the age specified in Paragraph A of this trust; or

(3) The trust property is used up through distributions allowed under these provisions.

If the trust terminates because the beneficiary reaches the specified age, the remaining principal and accumulated net income of the trust shall pass to the beneficiary. If the trust terminates because the beneficiary dies, the remaining principal and accumulated net income of the trust shall pass to the trust beneficiary's heirs.

E. Powers of Trustee

In addition to other powers granted to the trustee in this will, the trustee shall have:

(1) All the powers generally conferred on trustees by the laws of the state having jurisdiction over this trust;

(2) With respect to property in the trust, the powers conferred by this will on the executor; and

(3) The authority to hire and pay from the trust assets the reasonable fees of investment advisors, accountants, tax advisors, agents, attorneys and other assistants to administer the trust and manage any trust asset and for any litigation affecting the trust.

F. Trust Administration Provisions

(1) This trust shall be administered independent of court supervision to the maximum extent possible under the laws of the state having jurisdiction over this trust.

(2) The interests of trust beneficiaries shall not be transferable by voluntary or involuntary assignment or by operation of law and shall be free from the claims of creditors and from attachment, execution, bankruptcy or other legal process to the fullest extent permissible by law.

(3) Any trustee serving shall be entitled to reasonable compensation out of the trust assets for ordinary and extraordinary services, and for all services in connection with the complete or partial termination of any trust created by this will.

(4) The invalidity of any provision of this trust instrument shall not affect the validity of the remaining provisions.

I subscribe my name to this will this __12th__ day of _September_ , 20_00_, at

___Essex County___, State of ___New Jersey___ , and declare it is my last will, that I sign it willingly, that I execute it as my free and voluntary act for the purposes expressed, and that I am of the age of majority or otherwise legally empowered to make a will and under no constraint or undue influence.

David Warfman
Signature

WITNESSES

On this _12th_ day of _September_, 20_00_, the testator _David Warfman_,
declared to us, the undersigned, that this instrument was his or her will and requested us to
act as witnesses to it. The testator signed this will in our presence, all of us being present at
the same time. We now, at the testator's request, in the testator's presence, and in the
presence of each other, subscribe our names as witnesses and each declare that we are of
sound mind and of proper age to witness a will. We further declare that we understand this to
be the testator's will, and that to the best of our knowledge the testator is of the age of
majority, or is otherwise legally empowered to make a will, and appears to be of sound mind
and under no constraint or undue influence.

We declare under penalty of perjury that the foregoing is true and
correct, this _12th_ day of _September_, 20_00_, at
Essex County, State of _New Jersey_.

John Stone	John Stone
witness's signature	typed or printed name

residing at _125 Main Street_, _Clifton_,
street address city / city

Essex, _New Jersey_.
county / state

Amanda Stone	Amanda Stone
witness's signature	typed or printed name

residing at _125 Main Street_, _Clifton_,
street address / city

Essex, _New Jersey_.
county / state

Douglas White	Douglas White
witness's signature	typed or printed name

residing at _200 Main Street_, _Clifton_,
street address / city

Essex, _New Jersey_.
county / state

AFFIDAVIT

STATE OF _____ New Jersey _____

COUNTY OF _____ Essex _____

    I, the undersigned, an officer authorized to administer oaths, certify that _____ David Warfman _____ the

testator, and _____ John Stone _____,

_____ Amanda Stone _____ and

_____ Douglas White _____, the witnesses, whose names are signed to the attached or foregoing instrument and whose signatures appear below, having appeared together before me and having been first duly sworn, each then declared to me that:

1)   the attached or foregoing instrument is the last will of the testator;

2)   the testator willingly and voluntarily declared, signed and executed the will in the presence of the witnesses;

3)   the witnesses signed the will upon request by the testator, in the presence and hearing of the testator, and in the presence of each other;

4)   to the best knowledge of each witness the testator was, at that time of the signing, of the age of majority (or otherwise legally competent to make a will), of sound mind, and under no constraint or undue influence; and

5)   each witness was and is competent, and of the proper age to witness a will.

Testator: _____ David Wharfman _____

Witness: _____ John Stone _____

Address: _____ 125 Main ST., Clifton, New Jersey _____

Witness: _____ Amanda Stone _____

Address: _____ 125 Main St., Clifton, New Jersey _____

Witness: _____ Douglas White _____

Address: _____ 200 Main St., Clifton, New Jersey _____

Subscribed, sworn and acknowledged before me, _____ Beth O'Neill _____,

a notary public, by _____ David Warfman _____,

the testator, and by _____ John Stone _____,

_____ Amanda Stone _____,

and _____ Douglas White _____,

the witnesses, this 12th day of September 2000.

                    SIGNED: _____ Beth O'Neill _____

[NOTARY SEAL]

                    _____ Notary Public, State of NJ _____

                        OFFICIAL CAPACITY OF OFFICER

F. Letters of Explanation

Your basic will does not explain why you've made your decisions. If you want to clarify your motives and intentions, the best way is to prepare a separate letter and store it along with your will. You can say anything you want in your letter and cover any issues that are vital to you. But make sure your letter doesn't contain anything that seems to (or does) conflict with any part of your will. And to guard against any possible misunderstanding in this regard, state in your letter that you know it is not a binding legal document and is not intended to be a part of your will.

Usually, letters of explanation are motivated by love, the desire to express, in writing, deep and caring feelings the will writer has. Here are some examples of concerns you may want to cover in a letter.

- *Unequal gifts.* If you've left more property to one person than another, you may want to explain why. For instance, parents might leave more money to a child who doesn't earn a lot, or less money to a child who has already received part of his or her inheritance. Or a parent may decide that one child's special health or educational needs warrant leaving that child more property than the other children. Doing this can raise serious family concerns—a child who receives less may conclude that you cared for him or her less. Explaining your reasons for your unequal distribution of property can help soothe wounded feelings.

- *Gifts to adults to use for children.* If you've left money or property to an adult, with the understanding that it's for the benefit of a child, you can clarify how you want the gift used. Although your wishes won't be legally binding, they'll go a long way in establishing that the money was for college, not a car.

- *Desires for your children's upbringing.* If you have named minor children in your will, you've prepared for the possibility that they may be raised by their personal guardian. This person most likely has a good sense of who you and your children are, and how you'd like them raised. Nevertheless, it can't hurt to state in a letter how you would like your children to be brought up.

- *Pets.* You can't use your will to legally put requirements on how your pets will be cared for. However, you can make your wishes known by letter, especially if you've left money to help pay for your pet's upkeep.

- *Funeral arrangements.* You may want to express your wishes about your funeral, memorial service, cremation, burial or organ donation. Be sure to give a copy of these instructions to another person; wills are often not discovered and dealt with until long after decisions about final disposition have been made.

Finally, one warning: Don't write anything libelous, such as words another person could reasonably regard as untrue and insulting. I won't bore you with the technical definitions of libel. What it means, in commonsense terms, is that a letter (or a will for that matter) is not a place to seek revenge or express anger in a written attack. If someone proves in court that your will libeled him or her, your estate would be held responsible.

SAMPLE LETTER OF EXPLANATION

December 16, 2001

To my executor and my children:

This letter expresses my feelings and reasons for certain decisions I made in my will. I know that this letter is not my will, nor do I intend it to be an interpretation of my will. My will, which was signed by me, dated and witnessed on December 10, 2001, is the sole expression of my intentions concerning all my property, and other matters covered in that will.

I am giving the bulk of my property to my son John for one reason: because of his health problems, he needs it more. I love my other children, Ted and Ellen, just as much, and I am extremely proud of the life choices they have made. But I believe the truth is that they can manage fine without a substantial inheritance from me, but John is unlikely to be able to do so.

I request that my executor give a copy of this letter to each person mentioned in this letter, and to anyone else my executor determines should receive a copy.

Sincerely,

Lee Monroe ■

CHAPTER 9

Storing and Copying Your Will

Once your will is properly signed and witnessed, your work is essentially done. There are only a couple of small matters left to deal with. Happily, neither of these tasks entails much time or effort.

A. Storing Your Will

Your will should be easy to locate at your death. You don't want your executor, or your loved ones, to undergo the hassles of having to search for your will when they are already dealing with the grief of losing you. Here are some suggestions.

- Staple the pages of your will together. That will prevent any pages from getting lost or misplaced.

- Place your signed and witnessed will in an envelope on which you have typed or printed the words "Will of (Your Name)."

- If you've prepared a self-proving affidavit, make sure it's stapled to your will. If you've written any letters explaining your decisions and wishes, place them in the envelope with your will.

- It's best to store the envelope in a fireproof metal box, file cabinet or home safe. A bank's safe deposit box in your name isn't a good place to store your will. Banks usually won't open a safe deposit box for someone other than the owner without a court order. In some states, such as Ohio and Texas, the local court clerk's office stores wills for a small fee; check with the clerk for details.

- Make sure your executor and at least one other person you trust know where to find your will.

B. Making Copies of Your Will

You may want to make photocopies of your original, signed will. A copy of your will is simply a photocopy of the original document that has been signed and witnessed. These photocopies are not legal duplicate originals, because you and your witnesses have not directly signed these copies. The original will is going to be needed for the probate process.

Many people choose to give a copy of their signed will to their executor, but no one else. They figure the executor will be in a better position to handle the job if she or he knows in advance what's involved. Others go further and choose to also give copies to their main beneficiaries, the principle being the more openness, the better.

There is no requirement that you distribute copies of your will; your will is your own business. You don't have to reveal its contents to anyone, even your witnesses.

Giving close family members or other loved ones a copy of your will may be a good idea if all relationships are amicable, but sadly there are sometimes practical reasons not to do so. If you worry that there could be controversy or conflict if you reveal your will to your beneficiaries, don't do it. But although not doing so resolves the matter while you are alive, it does not address problems that might arise after your death, when the contents of your will become known. If you think some family members or other (would-be) beneficiaries may be so disturbed that she, he or they might sue to have your will invalidated, you need to see a lawyer. But if the worst you can reasonably foresee is disgruntlement and hurt feelings—well, it's too bad, but it can't, in itself, have any effect on the validity of your will.

Some people are tempted to make more than one original of their will. This means photocopying the original will before it is signed and witnessed, and then having each document signed and witnessed. While it is legal in most states to prepare and sign duplicate original wills, it is never a good idea. Common sense tells you why: If you later decide to revoke your will or change it by adding a codicil, you'd have to locate and revoke each original. Tracking down all original versions of your will can be quite a burden. Or, worse, you might forget one of the duplicate original wills, and wind up changing or revoking some but not all, thus creating a confusing mess and potentially a legal disaster. ■

CHAPTER 10

Changing or Revoking Your Will

Once you've prepared your formal will using *The Quick and Legal Will Book,* it's extremely important that you not alter it by inserting handwritten or typed additions or changes. You cannot simply cross out something in your will, or write in a change. Doing so very probably invalidates your entire will.

If you decide you want to change or revoke your will, you must do so in a legally permitted manner. The laws of most states require that any additions or changes in a signed and witnessed will, even clerical ones, be done by following the same signing and witnessing requirements as for an original will.

A. When to Make a New Will

Major life changes usually require revoking the old will and preparing a new one. What kind of changes? Marriage or divorce or having a new child are the clearest examples. Some simple changes, say naming a new alternate beneficiary for a gift, can be accomplished by using a codicil—a written amendment to the terms of a will. (This is discussed in Section B, below.)

To prepare a new will, you can follow the instructions in this book to prepare a will that reflects your current will writing wishes. If you had your will word processed, it should be very easy to update and prepare a new one and have it signed and witnessed. Be sure to destroy all old wills by tearing them up and tossing the pieces out.

Let's look at some occurrences that signal you should make a new will.

1. If Your Marital Status Changes

Suppose that after you've completed your will you get married. Or suppose you've prepared your will, leaving all or part of your property to your spouse, and you get divorced. As I've discussed, in most states a spouse has legal rights to the other spouse's property on death. And under the laws in many states, a divorce automatically cancels a gift to an ex-spouse. The alternate beneficiary named for that gift, or, if there is none, the residuary beneficiary, gets the property. In some states, however, an ex-spouse would still inherit as directed in the will. If you remarry, state legal rules become even more murky.

Rather than try to deal with all these complexities, follow this simple rule: Make a new will if you marry, divorce or if you are separated and seriously considering divorce.

2. If You Have or Adopt Additional Children

Each time a child is born or legally adopted into your family, make a new will. In the new will, you will list all of your children, and provide for them according to your wishes. If you do not do this, a child might later challenge your will in court, claiming that he or she was overlooked as an heir and is entitled to a substantial share of your property.

3. If Your Property Situation Changes Significantly

If the property you leave in your will either expands or shrinks significantly after you've made out your will, you should review your will to make sure it realistically reflects your current situation. If it doesn't, make a new will. This is especially important if there are changes in your ownership of real estate or expensive personal property items. For example, if you leave your 1988 Cadillac to your son and then trade it in and buy a 1995 Buick, your son won't get your wheels unless you update your will. On the other hand, if you leave your son "my car," he'll get whatever car you own at your death, even if it's a different one than you owned when you made your will. And if you own two cars at your death, there'll be confusion as to which car you meant to leave to your son. So once you acquire the second car, you'd need to revise your will to reflect that fact. (This could be done by codicil. See Section B, below.)

4. If You Move to a Different State

First the good news: a will valid in the state where it was made remains valid if you move to a new state. So the fact that you've moved to new state, in itself, doesn't necessitate preparing a new will.

Now, the exception: If you are married and move from a community property state to a common law state (see Chapter 3, Property Ownership, Section E), and your existing will does not leave half your property to your spouse, make a new will that does leave your spouse at least half of your property. Remember, this is required by law in common law states.

5. If Any of Your Beneficiaries Die

If a beneficiary you have named to receive a significant amount of property (either as a specific or residuary beneficiary) dies before you, you should make a new will. It is most important to do this if you named only one beneficiary for the gift and did not name an alternate— or if the alternate you named is no longer your first choice to get the property.

6. If Your Children's Personal Guardian, Property Manager or Trustee of a Children's Trust Cannot Serve

The first choice or alternate named to serve as a personal or property guardian for your minor children or trustee for their property left in a children's trust may move away, become disabled or turn out to be unsuitable for the job. If so, you'll likely want to make a new will naming somebody else.

7. If Your Executor Cannot Serve

The executor of your estate is responsible for making sure your will provisions are carried out. If you decide that the executor you named originally is no longer suitable, name another. (This can be done either in a new will or by codicil.)

8. Other Reasons for Preparing a New Will

You should prepare a new will if:

- you change your mind about who you want to receive significant portions of your property, or
- any of your children die before you, leaving children of their own. In some states, these children (your grandchildren) may be entitled to receive a share of your estate—unless they receive property under the will or you've specifically disinherited them.

B. Making Simple Changes in Your Will by Codicil

You can make simple changes to your will by means of a codicil—the legal name for a written amendment to the terms of a will, made after the original will has been witnessed and signed. Codicils are frequently used for small matters such as changes of individual gifts. In a codicil, the will writer can revoke a portion of the will he or she wants to change and then add a new clause, or the will writer can simply add a new provision, such as making a new specific personal property gift.

A codicil, being a sort of legal "P.S." to the will, must be executed with all of the formalities of a will that were discussed in Chapter 8, Preparing Your Final Will. This means that the codicil must be typed or word processed, then dated and signed by you in front of two or three witnesses. These witnesses don't have to be the same people who witnessed the will, but it's advisable to use them if they're available. As with your original witnesses, they must not be named as beneficiaries in your will. If your will is "self-proved" with a notarized affidavit, another affidavit for the codicil should also be executed. Once the codicil is completed, it should be stored with the original will.

A codicil form is provided in the Appendix. But let me remind you again: For major revisions, don't use a codicil. Instead, draft a new will and revoke the old one. A will that has been substantially rewritten by codicil is a confusing document and difficult to understand. It may not be clear what the relationship of the codicil to the original will provision means.

Here are some examples of the kinds of simple changes that can be accomplished by codicil.

Example 1: *Juliette changes banks for her sole account. She has identified her previous bank in a specific gift in her will, so she prepares the following codicil.*

First: I revoke the provision of Section 3 of my will that provided I leave my bank account at First City Bank, Chicago, Illinois, to Patsy Vieren.

Second: I add the following provision to Section 3 of my will:

I leave my bank account at the Chicago Merchant's Bank and Trust, Chicago, Illinois, to Patsy Vieren.

Example 2: *John's (the will writer) brother, Jim, has died. John now wants to leave the player piano he'd left to Jim to Jim's son, Fred. Here's the codicil John executes.*

First: I revoke the provision of Section 4 of my will that provided that I leave my player piano to my brother, Jim Baxter.

Second: I add the following provision to Section 4: I leave my player piano to my nephew, Fred Baxter.

Example 3: *Kendall has purchased two valuable stained glass lamps. She wants to leave them to her sister, Babs. There is nothing to delete from her old will, so she crosses out the first (deletion) clause of the codicil form. Then she adds the following codicil to her will.*

I add the following provision to Section 3 of my will:

I leave my two stained glass lamps from the 1900s to my sister, Babs Zelinsky, or, if she does not survive me, to my niece, Letitia Moore.

Be sure anyone with a copy of your will receives a copy of the codicil. This may be a nuisance, but will prevent confusion, or even conflict, later. The codicil doesn't have to be made part of the signature page of the original will. It must, however, refer to that will. This can be simply accomplished by labeling the codicil document "first codicil of the will of ___[your name]___, dated ___[give date will was originally prepared]___." The entire will is now considered to have been prepared as of the date of the codicil.

Don't prepare more than one codicil. If you need to make further changes in your will, prepare a new will. Having two or more codicils can lead to confusion regarding what's in or out of your will.

C. Revoking Your Will

Anyone who writes a will should understand how it can be revoked. There are only two ways: first, by deliberate act of the will writer; second, by operation of law. Let's look at each of these.

1. Deliberate Act to Revoke a Will

A will writer who wants to revoke a prior will should do so by express written statement in his or her new will. All the will forms in this book provide that the will writer revokes any previous wills.

Many states' laws provide that an existing will (or codicil) is also revoked by being "burnt, torn, concealed, defaced, obliterated or destroyed" (or similar wording) if the will writer intended to revoke it. This can be legally accomplished by someone other than the will writer at his or her direction. The problem with destroying a will, or having someone else do so, is that this only serves to revoke the will if you intend it to. After your death, this can become a matter of controversy, especially if you've distributed copies of your original will. So if you want the satisfaction of destroying a revoked will, go right ahead, but to be secure, make certain you've also revoked it in writing in your new will.

2. Revocation of Will Provisions by Act of Law

As is discussed in Chapter 3, Property Ownership, Section E, a spouse in a common law state has a statutory right to a certain percentage of the other spouse's estate (unless that right has been waived by a written marital agreement). And, as discussed in Chapter 4, Children, Section C, children not mentioned in a will have statutory rights to a part of a parent's estate.

So the law looks upon the will as being revoked as far as a spouse not provided for or unmentioned children are concerned, but not as to any other provisions. With a will drafted from this book, you shouldn't have to concern yourself with this. If you followed the instructions, you've suitably provided for your spouse and mentioned all your children in your will, and have either given something to each of your children or disinherited them by not leaving them anything. ■

CHAPTER 11

Going Further

Some readers may decide they want to learn more about the options for will writing or explore estate planning concerns beyond what is offered in this book. Here I discuss other Nolo resources that provide information beyond the scope of this book. Finally, I cover some realistic points about hiring a lawyer.

A. Other Will Writing Options

Nolo's Will Book, by Denis Clifford, and Nolo's *WillMaker* (computer will program) offer many options for a will that are not included in this basic book. Both provide broader coverage of possible will issues, and give a more in-depth discussion of essential will matters. Additional issues covered in these resources include:

- *a debt-forgiveness clause.* One type of "gift" you can achieve by your will is to forgive debts owed to you. If you don't, the debt remains alive and the debtor will need to pay it to your estate.

- *a clause providing what estate resources are to be used to pay any last debts and taxes.* If you don't specify, this is normally decided by your executor.

- *a clause naming different personal guardians for different children.* In some situations, a will writer feels different personal guardians would be in the children's best interest.

- *a clause where you can state specific reasons why the personal guardian you've named for your children is the best choice.* This explanation may be persuasive in a variety of circumstances, particularly where a custodial parent objects to the other parent raising the children.

- *a clause where you can name different property guardians for different children.* Again, this is for situations where the will writer decides different property guardians would be in the children's best interest.

- *an express disinheritance clause.* This can be used by people who want to be explicit that someone (particularly a child) is intentionally excluded from receiving any property under the will. (This clause is available in *Nolo's Will Book* only.)

- *a clause covering mortgages on real estate.* If you leave some real estate (for example, a house) and don't mention anything about the mortgage on that property, the mortgage goes with the gift. This clause allows you to give the gift free of the mortgage, which must be paid off from other specified assets in your estate. (Only *Nolo's Will Book* covers this issue.)

- *options for adult management of property left to minors, other than a children's trust.* See sidebar, "The Uniform Transfers to Minors Act and a Family Pot Trust," below.

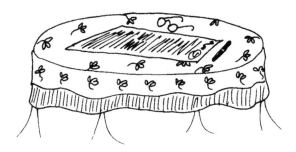

THE UNIFORM TRANSFERS TO MINORS ACT AND A FAMILY POT TRUST

In addition to a children's trust, there are two additional and important options for adult management of property left to minors.

The Uniform Transfers to Minors Act

The Uniform Transfers to Minors Act (UTMA) provides residents of most states with a convenient method for leaving property to a minor child. The UTMA is a model law proposed by a group of legal scholars who make up the Uniform Law Commission. The UTMA, with slight variations, has been adopted by legislators of all states, except Michigan, South Carolina and Vermont.

I haven't included information about how to use the UTMA in wills in states where it is legal because the aim of this book is to be, as its title suggests, both quick and legal. It won't be quick enough if I take you through the UTMA rules, and a child's trust works in every state.

Both the UTMA and a children's trust are effective, efficient methods for handling property left to minors. With the UTMA, you name a "custodian" to manage property you've left to the minor until he or she reaches a set age, usually 21 (it can range from 18 to 25, depending on state law). The custodian's duties and responsibilities are defined in each state's UTMA. Generally, the custodian can act freely in the best interests of the child. The UTMA can be a very handy method for leaving property to a minor, as it requires very little paperwork. The UTMA is particularly attractive where a gift is likely to be used up by the time the minor is 21—say for college costs. This UTMA option is available in both *Nolo's Will Book* and Nolo's *WillMaker* computer program.

A FAMILY POT TRUST

With a pot trust, you place property left to different children in one trust (thus the term "pot"). The trustee has authority to use all property in the trust as he or she decides is best. In the children's trusts in the will forms in this book, one child's trust property, or income from that property, may not be used for the benefit of another child. By contrast, in a family pot trust, the trustee could spend twice as much money for one child as for another. Thus the appeal of a pot trust: it permits the trustee maximum flexibility to use any property left for children's benefit as that trustee deems correct.

The possible downside is that one child beneficiary could have little or no trust money spent for his or her benefit, and wind up with nothing when the trust ends, because all trust property was spent for some other family member. A family pot trust lasts until the youngest child reaches the age set for termination of the trust. It often involves difficult tax accounting problems and complex personal problems for the trustee, who must choose how to distribute the trust property among the children. (A family pot trust, for families whose children are all minors, is available in both *Nolo's Will Book* and Nolo's *WillMaker*.)

B. For General Information on Estate Planning

Plan Your Estate, by Denis Clifford and Cora Jordan (Nolo Press), discusses all significant issues of estate planning and provides information relevant to all sizes of estates, from the very modest to the very wealthy. Anyone concerned with estate tax savings or probate avoidance methods will benefit from reading this book. Even if you eventually decide you need to see a lawyer, reading *Plan Your Estate* will help you become an educated consumer, so you can evaluate whether you're getting your money's worth.

C. Probate-Avoiding Living Trusts

I discussed reasons to avoid probate in Chapter 6, Estate Planning, Sections A and B. If you decide you want to further investigate creating a living trust to avoid probate, Nolo provides you with two choices: *Make Your Own Living Trust,* by Denis Clifford, and Nolo's *Living Trust Maker* (living trust computer program). Both provide thorough explanations of what a living trust is and does. Both also provide the information and forms to allow you to create your own living trust.

D. Creating an "AB" or Marital Life Estate Trust for Estate Tax Savings

Make Your Own Living Trust provides the information and forms you can use to create one type of AB trust. The type of trust offered in *Make Your Own Living Trust* is for couples with combined net estates over the estate tax threshold. (See Chapter 6, Estate Planning, Section C.)

E. Creating a Durable Power of Attorney for Health Care

Nolo's *WillMaker* (computer program) has one component that allows you to create your own durable power of attorney for health care document. This form is specifically geared to be valid under your state's laws. A durable power of attorney for health care, as discussed in Chapter 6, Estate Planning, Section F, is a legally-binding document where you authorize someone else to make medical/health care decisions for you, or enforce your specific instructions, if you become incompetent and unable to make or enforce your own decisions.

The document in *WillMaker* is limited to carrying out your wishes for health care if you are terminally ill and unable to express your wishes at the time, or if you are in a permanent coma. It is not appropriate for other contexts, where you might wish to have someone make your health care decisions for you, such as if you develop Alzheimer's disease or become mentally ill.

F. Creating a Durable Power of Attorney for Finances

You can create a durable power of attorney for finances using either Nolo's *WillMaker,* or *The Financial Power of Attorney Workbook,* by Shae Irving (Nolo Press).

G. Using Lawyers

While this book is designed for do-it-yourself preparation of your own basic will, there will certainly be some readers who discover that they want to see a lawyer. Here I discuss when that is feasible or needed.

1. Hiring a Lawyer to Review Your Will

Hiring a lawyer solely to review the will you've prepared sounds like a good idea. It shouldn't cost much, and seems to offer a comforting security. Sadly, though, it may be difficult or even impossible to find a lawyer who will accept the job.

While this is unfortunate, I'm not willing to excoriate lawyers who won't review a do-it-yourself will. From their point of view, they are being asked to accept what can turn into a significant responsibility for what they regard as inadequate compensation, given their usual fees. Any prudent lawyer sees every client as a potential occasion for a malpractice claim, or at least, serious later hassles—a phone call four years down the line that begins, "We talked to you about our wills, and now…." Many experienced lawyers want to avoid this kind of risk. Also, many lawyers feel that if they're only reviewing someone else's work, they simply don't get deeply enough into a situation to be sure of their opinions. All you can do here is to keep trying to find a sympathetic lawyer—or be prepared to pay enough that the lawyer can feel she has been compensated adequately to review your will.

2. Situations Where You'll Need a Lawyer

There are certainly instances where you will need to hire a lawyer for assistance in will writing/estate planning. Some common situations are where:

- you want a special needs trust for a disadvantaged child or family member

- you think someone will contest your will

- you're in a second or subsequent marriage where at least one spouse has children from a prior marriage, and you have concerns that there may be conflict between your spouse and your children over your property disposition

- your individual estate exceeds the federal estate tax threshold

- you and your spouse's combined estate is over the federal estate tax threshold and you decide you do not want to create an AB trust from *Make Your Own Living Trust*

- you and your spouse's combined estate exceeds $1,200,000, or

- you want to put restrictions on your gifts, such as controlling how long one beneficiary has use of it before the property goes to another beneficiary.

This is not an exhaustive list, of course. When human beings, property, love and other emotions, death and law all intersect, the possibilities for complexities (and pain) are endless.

If you want a discussion of how to find a lawyer, check any of the Nolo resources listed in this chapter. Here I don't cover in depth how to find a lawyer if you need one. Most readers simply won't need a lawyer. If you do, asking around is the best route. Try to find someone who's used a lawyer for a will or estate plan and is satisfied with what she or he got. Ask friends, work associates and anyone you know who's in business for themselves—this will often yield at least a referral to a reliable will/estate planning lawyer.

If you see a lawyer, I urge you—double urge you—not to be intimidated. Be sure you feel at ease with the lawyer, and that he or she is willing to work *with* you (not just tell you he or she has "finished" your work) and gives you a clear estimate of his or her charges for the work.

Let me conclude by reminding you that if your desires are clear and your situation straightforward, you can, as I've been reiterating throughout this book, safely prepare your will on your own. ∎

Appendix

Form 1. Married With Child(ren), Property to Spouse

Will of _____

I, _____,
a resident of _____, State of _____.
declare that this is my will.

1. Revocation. I revoke all wills that I have previously made.

2. Marital Status. I am married to _____.

3. Children. I have the following child(ren):

Name	Date of Birth
_____	_____
_____	_____
_____	_____

If I do not leave property to one or more of the children or grandchildren whom I have identified above, my failure to do so is intentional.

4. Specific Gifts. I make the following specific gifts of property:
I leave _____
_____
_____
to _____
or, if such beneficiary(ies) do(es) not survive me, to _____
_____.

I leave _____
_____
_____
to _____
or, if such beneficiary(ies) do(es) not survive me, to _____
_____.

I leave _____

_____

_____

to _____

or, if such beneficiary(ies) do(es) not survive me, to _____

_____.

Any specific gift made in this will to two or more beneficiaries shall be shared equally among them, unless unequal shares are specifically indicated. All shared gifts must be sold, and the net proceeds distributed as the will directs, unless all beneficiaries for that gift agree in writing, after the will writer's death, that the gift need not be sold.

If I name two or more primary beneficiaries to receive a specific gift of property and any of them do not survive me, all surviving primary beneficiaries shall equally divide the deceased primary beneficiary's share unless I have specifically provided otherwise. If I name two or more alternate beneficiaries to receive a specific gift of property and any of them do not survive me, all surviving alternate beneficiaries shall equally divide the deceased alternate beneficiary's share.

5. Residuary Estate. I leave my residuary estate, that is, the rest of my property not otherwise specifically and validly disposed of by this will or in any other manner, to my spouse, _____, or, if my spouse does not survive me, to my child(ren), _____

_____.

If I name two or more children as alternate residuary beneficiaries to receive property and any of them do not survive me, all surviving alternate residuary beneficiaries shall equally divide the deceased alternate residuary beneficiary's share.

As used in any section of this will, the word "survive" means to outlive the will writer by at least 45 days.

6. Executor. I name _____ as executor, to serve without bond. If that executor does not qualify, or ceases to serve, I name _____ as executor, also to serve without bond.

I direct that my executor take all actions legally permissible to probate this will, including filing a petition in the appropriate court for the independent administration of my estate.

I grant to my executor the following powers, to be exercised as the executor deems to be in the best interests of my estate:

(1) To retain property, without liability for loss or depreciation resulting from such retention.

(2) To sell, lease or exchange property and to receive or administer the proceeds as a part of my estate.

(3) To vote stock, convert bonds, notes, stocks or other securities belonging to my estate into other securities, and to exercise all other rights and privileges of a person owning similar property.

(4) To deal with and settle claims in favor of or against my estate.

(5) To continue, maintain, operate or participate in any business which is a part of my estate, and to incorporate, dissolve or otherwise change the form of organization of the business.

(6) To pay all debts and taxes that may be assessed against my estate, as provided under state law.

(7) To do all other acts, which in the executor's judgment may be necessary or appropriate for the proper and advantageous management, investment and distribution of my estate.

These powers, authority and discretion are in addition to the powers, authority and discretion vested in an executor by operation of law, and may be exercised as often as deemed necessary, without approval by any court in any jurisdiction.

7. Personal Guardian. If at my death any of my children are minors and a personal guardian is needed, I name _____
as the personal guardian, to serve without bond. If this person is unable or unwilling to serve as personal guardian, I name _____
as personal guardian, also to serve without bond.

8. Property Guardian. If any of my children are minors and a property guardian is needed, I name _____
as the property guardian, to serve without bond. If this person is unable or unwilling to serve as property guardian, I name _____
as property guardian, also to serve without bond.

Form 1

9. Children's Trust. All property I leave in this will to any of the beneficiaries listed in Section A, below, shall be held for each of them in a separate trust, administered according to the following terms:

A. Trust Beneficiaries and Age Limits

Each trust shall end when the following beneficiaries become 35 years of age, except as otherwise specified in this section.

Trust Beneficiary	Trust Shall End At Age
_____	_____
_____	_____
_____	_____
_____	_____
_____	_____

B. Trustees

I name _____
as trustee, to serve without bond. If this person is unable or unwilling to serve as trustee, I name _____
as successor trustee, also to serve without bond.

C. Beneficiary Provisions

(1) The trustee may distribute for the benefit of each beneficiary as much of the net income or principal of the trust as the trustee deems necessary for the beneficiary's health, support, maintenance and education. In deciding whether to make a distribution for or to a beneficiary, the trustee may take into account the beneficiary's other income, resources and sources of support.

(2) Any trust income that is not distributed to a beneficiary by the trustee shall be accumulated and added to the principal of the trust administered for that beneficiary.

D. Termination of Trust

The trust shall terminate when any of the following occurs:
(1) The beneficiary becomes the age specified in Paragraph A of this trust;
(2) The beneficiary dies before becoming the age specified in Paragraph A of this trust; or
(3) The trust property is used up through distributions allowed under these provisions.

If the trust terminates because the beneficiary reaches the specified age, the remaining principal and accumulated net income of the trust shall pass to the beneficiary. If the trust terminates because the beneficiary dies, the remaining principal and accumulated net income of the trust shall pass to the trust beneficiary's heirs.

E. Powers of Trustee

In addition to other powers granted to the trustee in this will, the trustee shall have:

(1) All the powers generally conferred on trustees by the laws of the state having jurisdiction over this trust;

(2) With respect to property in the trust, the powers conferred by this will on the executor; and

(3) The authority to hire and pay from the trust assets the reasonable fees of investment advisors, accountants, tax advisors, agents, attorneys and other assistants to administer the trust and manage any trust asset and for any litigation affecting the trust.

F. Trust Administration Provisions

(1) This trust shall be administered independent of court supervision to the maximum extent possible under the laws of the state having jurisdiction over this trust.

(2) The interests of trust beneficiaries shall not be transferable by voluntary or involuntary assignment or by operation of law and shall be free from the claims of creditors and from attachment, execution, bankruptcy or other legal process to the fullest extent permissible by law.

(3) Any trustee serving shall be entitled to reasonable compensation out of the trust assets for ordinary and extraordinary services, and for all services in connection with the complete or partial termination of any trust created by this will.

(4) The invalidity of any provision of this trust instrument shall not affect the validity of the remaining provisions.

I subscribe my name to this will this _____ day of _____, 20__, at _____, State of _____, and declare it is my will, that I sign it willingly, that I execute it as my free and voluntary act for the purposes expressed, and that I am of the age of majority or otherwise legally empowered to make a will and under no constraint or undue influence.

_____
signature

Form 1

Witnesses

On this _____ day of _____, 20 ___, the testator,

_____, declared to us, the

undersigned, that this instrument was his or her will and requested us to act as witnesses to

it. The testator signed this will in our presence, all of us being present at the same time. We

now, at the testator's request, in the testator's presence, and in the presence of each other,

subscribe our names as witnesses and each declare that we are of sound mind and of proper

age to witness a will. We further declare that we understand this to be the testator's will, and

that to the best of our knowledge the testator is of the age of majority, or is otherwise legally

empowered to make a will, and appears to be of sound mind and under no constraint or

undue influence.

We declare under penalty of perjury that the foregoing is true and correct, this _____

day of _____, 20 ___, at _____,

State of _____.

_____   _____
witness's signature   typed or printed name

residing at _____, _____,
street address   city

_____, _____.
county   state

_____   _____
witness's signature   typed or printed name

residing at _____, _____,
street address   city

_____, _____.
county   state

_____   _____
witness's signature   typed or printed name

residing at _____, _____,
street address   city

_____, _____.
county   state

Form 2. Married With No Children

Will of _____

I, _____,
a resident of _____, State of _____,
declare that this is my will.

1. Revocation. I revoke all wills that I have previously made.

2. Marital Status. I am married to _____.

3. Specific Gifts. I make the following specific gifts of property:
I leave _____
_____
_____
to _____
or, if such beneficiary(ies) do(es) not survive me, to _____
_____.

I leave _____
_____
_____
to _____
or, if such beneficiary(ies) do(es) not survive me, to _____
_____.

I leave _____
_____
_____
to _____
or, if such beneficiary(ies) do(es) not survive me, to _____
_____.

I leave _____
_____
_____

to _____

or, if such beneficiary(ies) do(es) not survive me, to _____

_____ .

Any specific gift made in this will to two or more beneficiaries shall be shared equally among them, unless unequal shares are specifically indicated. All shared gifts must be sold, and the net proceeds distributed as the will directs, unless all beneficiaries for that gift agree in writing, after the will writer's death, that the gift need not be sold.

If I name two or more primary beneficiaries to receive a specific gift of property and any of them do not survive me, all surviving primary beneficiaries shall equally divide the deceased primary beneficiary's share unless I have specifically provided otherwise. If I name two or more alternate beneficiaries to receive a specific gift of property and any of them do not survive me, all surviving alternate beneficiaries shall equally divide the deceased alternate beneficiary's share.

4. Residuary Estate. I leave my residuary estate, that is, the rest of my property not otherwise specifically and validly disposed of by this will or in any other manner, to

_____ or, if such residuary

beneficiary(ies) do(es) not survive me, to _____

_____ .

Any residuary gift made in this will to two or more beneficiaries shall be shared equally among them, unless unequal shares are specifically indicated. All shared residuary gifts must be sold, and the net proceeds distributed as the will directs, unless all beneficiaries for that gift agree in writing, after the will writer's death, that the gift need not be sold.

If I name two or more alternate residuary beneficiaries to receive property and any of them do not survive me, all surviving alternate residuary beneficiaries shall equally divide the deceased alternate residuary beneficiary's share.

As used in any section of this will, the word "survive" means to outlive the will writer by at least 45 days.

5. Executor. I name _____

as executor, to serve without bond. If that executor does not qualify, or ceases to serve, I name _____

as executor, also to serve without bond.

I direct that my executor take all actions legally permissible to probate this will, including filing a petition in the appropriate court for the independent administration of my estate.

I grant to my executor the following powers, to be exercised as the executor deems to be in the best interests of my estate:

(1) To retain property, without liability for loss or depreciation resulting from such retention.

(2) To sell, lease or exchange property and to receive or administer the proceeds as a part of my estate.

(3) To vote stock, convert bonds, notes, stocks or other securities belonging to my estate into other securities, and to exercise all other rights and privileges of a person owning similar property.

(4) To deal with and settle claims in favor of or against my estate.

(5) To continue, maintain, operate or participate in any business which is a part of my estate, and to incorporate, dissolve or otherwise change the form of organization of the business.

(6) To pay all debts and taxes that may be assessed against my estate, as provided under state law.

(7) To do all other acts, which in the executor's judgment may be necessary or appropriate for the proper and advantageous management, investment and distribution of my estate.

These powers, authority and discretion are in addition to the powers, authority and discretion vested in an executor by operation of law, and may be exercised as often as deemed necessary, without approval by any court in any jurisdiction.

I subscribe my name to this will this _____ day of _____, 20 ___, at _____, State of _____, and declare it is my will, that I sign it willingly, that I execute it as my free and voluntary act for the purposes expressed, and that I am of the age of majority or otherwise legally empowered to make a will and under no constraint or undue influence.

_____
signature

Form 2

Witnesses

On this _____ day of _____, 20 ___, the testator,
_____, declared to us, the
undersigned, that this instrument was his or her will and requested us to act as witnesses to
it. The testator signed this will in our presence, all of us being present at the same time. We
now, at the testator's request, in the testator's presence, and in the presence of each other,
subscribe our names as witnesses and each declare that we are of sound mind and of proper
age to witness a will. We further declare that we understand this to be the testator's will, and
that to the best of our knowledge the testator is of the age of majority, or is otherwise legally
empowered to make a will, and appears to be of sound mind and under no constraint or
undue influence.

We declare under penalty of perjury that the foregoing is true and correct, this _____
day of _____, 20 ___, at _____,
State of _____.

_____   _____
witness's signature   typed or printed name

residing at _____, _____,
                 street address   city

_____, _____.
county   state

_____   _____
witness's signature   typed or printed name

residing at _____, _____,
                 street address   city

_____, _____.
county   state

_____   _____
witness's signature   typed or printed name

residing at _____, _____,
                 street address   city

_____, _____.
county   state

Form 3. Single, Divorced or Widowed With Child(ren)

Will of _____

I, _____,
a resident of _____, State of _____,
declare that this is my will.

1. Revocation. I revoke all wills that I have previously made.

2. Marital Status. I am not married.

3. Children. I have the following child(ren):

Name	Date of Birth

If I do not leave property to one or more of the children or grandchildren whom I have identified above, my failure to do so is intentional.

4. Specific Gifts. I make the following specific gifts of property:
I leave _____
_____
to _____
or, if such beneficiary(ies) do(es) not survive me, to _____
_____.

I leave _____
_____
to _____
or, if such beneficiary(ies) do(es) not survive me, to _____
_____.

I leave _____
_____

to _____

or, if such beneficiary(ies) do(es) not survive me, to _____

_____.

    I leave _____

_____

to _____

or, if such beneficiary(ies) do(es) not survive me, to _____

_____.

    Any specific gift made in this will to two or more beneficiaries shall be shared equally among them, unless unequal shares are specifically indicated. All shared gifts must be sold, and the net proceeds distributed as the will directs, unless all beneficiaries for that gift agree in writing, after the will writer's death, that the gift need not be sold.

    If I name two or more primary beneficiaries to receive a specific gift of property and any of them do not survive me, all surviving primary beneficiaries shall equally divide the deceased primary beneficiary's share unless I have specifically provided otherwise. If I name two or more alternate beneficiaries to receive a specific gift of property and any of them do not survive me, all surviving alternate beneficiaries shall equally divide the deceased alternate beneficiary's share.

    5. Residuary Estate. I leave my residuary estate, that is, the rest of my property not otherwise specifically and validly disposed of by this will or in any other manner, to

_____ or, if such residuary beneficiary(ies) do(es) not survive me, to _____

_____.

    Any residuary gift made in this will to two or more beneficiaries shall be shared equally among them, unless unequal shares are specifically indicated. All shared residuary gifts must be sold, and the net proceeds distributed as the will directs, unless all beneficiaries for that gift agree in writing, after the will writer's death, that the gift need not be sold.

    If I name two or more alternate residuary beneficiaries to receive property and any of them do not survive me, all surviving alternate residuary beneficiaries shall equally divide the deceased alternate residuary beneficiary's share.

    As used in any section of this will, the word "survive" means to outlive the will writer by at least 45 days.

    6. Executor. I name _____

as executor, to serve without bond. If that executor does not qualify, or ceases to serve, I name _____

as executor, also to serve without bond.

I direct that my executor take all actions legally permissible to probate this will, including filing a petition in the appropriate court for the independent administration of my estate.

I grant to my executor the following powers, to be exercised as the executor deems to be in the best interests of my estate:

(1) To retain property, without liability for loss or depreciation resulting from such retention.

(2) To sell, lease or exchange property and to receive or administer the proceeds as a part of my estate.

(3) To vote stock, convert bonds, notes, stocks or other securities belonging to my estate into other securities, and to exercise all other rights and privileges of a person owning similar property.

(4) To deal with and settle claims in favor of or against my estate.

(5) To continue, maintain, operate or participate in any business which is a part of my estate, and to incorporate, dissolve or otherwise change the form of organization of the business.

(6) To pay all debts and taxes that may be assessed against my estate, as provided under state law.

(7) To do all other acts, which in the executor's judgment may be necessary or appropriate for the proper and advantageous management, investment and distribution of my estate.

These powers, authority and discretion are in addition to the powers, authority and discretion vested in an executor by operation of law, and may be exercised as often as deemed necessary, without approval by any court in any jurisdiction.

7. Personal Guardian. If at my death any of my children are minors and a personal guardian is needed, I name _____

as the personal guardian, to serve without bond. If this person is unable or unwilling to serve as personal guardian, I name _____

as personal guardian, also to serve without bond.

8. Property Guardian. If any of my children are minors and a property guardian is needed, I name _____

as the property guardian, to serve without bond. If this person is unable or unwilling to

serve as property guardian, I name _____
as property guardian, also to serve without bond.

9. Children's Trust. All property I leave in this will to any of the beneficiaries listed in Section A, below, shall be held for each of them in a separate trust, administered according to the following terms:

A. Trust Beneficiaries and Age Limits

Each trust shall end when the following beneficiaries become 35 years of age, except as otherwise specified in this section.

Trust Beneficiary	Trust Shall End At Age
_____	_____
_____	_____
_____	_____
_____	_____
_____	_____

B. Trustees

I name _____
as trustee, to serve without bond. If this person is unable or unwilling to serve as trustee, I name _____
as successor trustee, also to serve without bond.

C. Beneficiary Provisions

(1) The trustee may distribute for the benefit of each beneficiary as much of the net income or principal of the trust as the trustee deems necessary for the beneficiary's health, support, maintenance and education. In deciding whether to make a distribution for or to a beneficiary, the trustee may take into account the beneficiary's other income, resources and sources of support.

(2) Any trust income that is not distributed to a beneficiary by the trustee shall be accumulated and added to the principal of the trust administered for that beneficiary.

D. Termination of Trust

The trust shall terminate when any of the following occurs:

(1) The beneficiary becomes the age specified in Paragraph A of this trust;

(2) The beneficiary dies before becoming the age specified in Paragraph A of this trust; or

(3) The trust property is used up through distributions allowed under these provisions.

If the trust terminates because the beneficiary reaches the specified age, the remaining principal and accumulated net income of the trust shall pass to the beneficiary. If the trust terminates because the beneficiary dies, the remaining principal and accumulated net income of the trust shall pass to the trust beneficiary's heirs.

E. Powers of Trustee

In addition to other powers granted to the trustee in this will, the trustee shall have:

(1) All the powers generally conferred on trustees by the laws of the state having jurisdiction over this trust;

(2) With respect to property in the trust, the powers conferred by this will on the executor; and

(3) The authority to hire and pay from the trust assets the reasonable fees of investment advisors, accountants, tax advisors, agents, attorneys and other assistants to administer the trust and manage any trust asset and for any litigation affecting the trust.

F. Trust Administration Provisions

(1) This trust shall be administered independent of court supervision to the maximum extent possible under the laws of the state having jurisdiction over this trust.

(2) The interests of trust beneficiaries shall not be transferable by voluntary or involuntary assignment or by operation of law and shall be free from the claims of creditors and from attachment, execution, bankruptcy or other legal process to the fullest extent permissible by law.

(3) Any trustee serving shall be entitled to reasonable compensation out of the trust assets for ordinary and extraordinary services, and for all services in connection with the complete or partial termination of any trust created by this will.

(4) The invalidity of any provision of this trust instrument shall not affect the validity of the remaining provisions.

I subscribe my name to this will this _____ day of _____, 20 ___, at _____, State of _____, and declare it is my will, that I sign it willingly, that I execute it as my free and voluntary act for the purposes expressed, and that I am of the age of majority or otherwise legally empowered to make a will and under no constraint or undue influence.

_____
signature

Form 3

Witnesses

On this _____ day of _____, 20___, the testator,

_____, declared to us, the undersigned, that this instrument was his or her will and requested us to act as witnesses to it. The testator signed this will in our presence, all of us being present at the same time. We now, at the testator's request, in the testator's presence, and in the presence of each other, subscribe our names as witnesses and each declare that we are of sound mind and of proper age to witness a will. We further declare that we understand this to be the testator's will, and that to the best of our knowledge the testator is of the age of majority, or is otherwise legally empowered to make a will, and appears to be of sound mind and under no constraint or undue influence.

We declare under penalty of perjury that the foregoing is true and correct, this _____ day of _____, 20___, at _____, State of _____.

_____   _____
witness's signature   typed or printed name

residing at _____, _____,
street address   city

_____, _____.
county   state

_____   _____
witness's signature   typed or printed name

residing at _____, _____,
street address   city

_____, _____.
county   state

_____   _____
witness's signature   typed or printed name

residing at _____, _____,
street address   city

_____, _____.
county   state

Form 4. Single, Divorced or Widowed With No Children

Will of _____

I, _____,
a resident of _____, State of _____,
declare that this is my will.

    1. Revocation. I revoke all wills that I have previously made.

    2. Marital Status. I am not married.

    3. Specific Gifts. I make the following specific gifts of property:
I leave _____
_____
_____
to _____
or, if such beneficiary(ies) do(es) not survive me, to _____
_____.

I leave _____
_____
_____
to _____
or, if such beneficiary(ies) do(es) not survive me, to _____
_____.

I leave _____
_____
_____
to _____
or, if such beneficiary(ies) do(es) not survive me, to _____
_____.

I leave _____
_____
_____

to _____

or, if such beneficiary(ies) do(es) not survive me, to _____

_____.

Any specific gift made in this will to two or more beneficiaries shall be shared equally among them, unless unequal shares are specifically indicated. All shared gifts must be sold, and the net proceeds distributed as the will directs, unless all beneficiaries for that gift agree in writing, after the will writer's death, that the gift need not be sold.

If I name two or more primary beneficiaries to receive a specific gift of property and any of them do not survive me, all surviving primary beneficiaries shall equally divide the deceased primary beneficiary's share unless I have specifically provided otherwise. If I name two or more alternate beneficiaries to receive a specific gift of property and any of them do not survive me, all surviving alternate beneficiaries shall equally divide the deceased alternate beneficiary's share.

4. Residuary Estate. I leave my residuary estate, that is, the rest of my property not otherwise specifically and validly disposed of by this will or in any other manner, to

_____ or, if such residuary

beneficiary(ies) do(es) not survive me, to _____

_____.

Any residuary gift made in this will to two or more beneficiaries shall be shared equally among them, unless unequal shares are specifically indicated. All shared residuary gifts must be sold, and the net proceeds distributed as the will directs, unless all beneficiaries for that gift agree in writing, after the will writer's death, that the gift need not be sold.

If I name two or more alternate residuary beneficiaries to receive property and any of them do not survive me, all surviving alternate residuary beneficiaries shall equally divide the deceased alternate residuary beneficiary's share.

As used in any section of this will, the word "survive" means to outlive the will writer by at least 45 days.

5. Executor. I name _____

as executor, to serve without bond. If that executor does not qualify, or ceases to serve, I name _____

as executor, also to serve without bond.

Form 4

I direct that my executor take all actions legally permissible to probate this will, including filing a petition in the appropriate court for the independent administration of my estate.

I grant to my executor the following powers, to be exercised as the executor deems to be in the best interests of my estate:

(1) To retain property, without liability for loss or depreciation resulting from such retention.

(2) To sell, lease or exchange property and to receive or administer the proceeds as a part of my estate.

(3) To vote stock, convert bonds, notes, stocks or other securities belonging to my estate into other securities, and to exercise all other rights and privileges of a person owning similar property.

(4) To deal with and settle claims in favor of or against my estate.

(5) To continue, maintain, operate or participate in any business which is a part of my estate, and to incorporate, dissolve or otherwise change the form of organization of the business.

(6) To pay all debts and taxes that may be assessed against my estate, as provided under state law.

(7) To do all other acts, which in the executor's judgment may be necessary or appropriate for the proper and advantageous management, investment and distribution of my estate.

These powers, authority and discretion are in addition to the powers, authority and discretion vested in an executor by operation of law, and may be exercised as often as deemed necessary, without approval by any court in any jurisdiction.

I subscribe my name to this will this _____ day of _____, 20____, at _____, State of _____, and declare it is my will, that I sign it willingly, that I execute it as my free and voluntary act for the purposes expressed, and that I am of the age of majority or otherwise legally empowered to make a will and under no constraint or undue influence.

_____
signature

Form 4

Witnesses

On this _____ day of _____, 20___, the testator,

_____, declared to us, the

undersigned, that this instrument was his or her will and requested us to act as witnesses to it. The testator signed this will in our presence, all of us being present at the same time. We now, at the testator's request, in the testator's presence, and in the presence of each other, subscribe our names as witnesses and each declare that we are of sound mind and of proper age to witness a will. We further declare that we understand this to be the testator's will, and that to the best of our knowledge the testator is of the age of majority, or is otherwise legally empowered to make a will, and appears to be of sound mind and under no constraint or undue influence.

We declare under penalty of perjury that the foregoing is true and correct, this _____

day of _____, 20___, at _____,

State of _____.

_____	_____
witness's signature	typed or printed name

residing at _____, _____,
　　　　　　　street address　　　　　　　　　　　city

_____, _____.
　　　county　　　　　　　　　　　　　state

_____	_____
witness's signature	typed or printed name

residing at _____, _____,
　　　　　　　street address　　　　　　　　　　　city

_____, _____.
　　　county　　　　　　　　　　　　　state

_____	_____
witness's signature	typed or printed name

residing at _____, _____,
　　　　　　　street address　　　　　　　　　　　city

_____, _____.
　　　county　　　　　　　　　　　　　state

Form 5. All-Purpose Will

Will of _____

I, _____,
a resident of _____ , State of _____,
declare that this is my will.

1. Revocation. I revoke all wills that I have previously made.

2. Marital Status. _____

3. Children. I have the following child(ren):

Name	Date of Birth
_____	_____
_____	_____
_____	_____

If I do not leave property to one or more of the children or grandchildren whom I have identified above, my failure to do so is intentional.

4. Specific Gifts. I make the following specific gifts of property:
I leave _____
_____
_____
to _____
or, if such beneficiary(ies) do(es) not survive me, to _____
_____.

I leave _____
_____
_____
to _____
or, if such beneficiary(ies) do(es) not survive me, to _____
_____.

I leave _____

_____

to _____

or, if such beneficiary(ies) do(es) not survive me, to _____

_____

I leave _____

_____

to _____

or, if such beneficiary(ies) do(es) not survive me, to _____

_____

Any specific gift made in this will to two or more beneficiaries shall be shared equally among them, unless unequal shares are specifically indicated. All shared gifts must be sold, and the net proceeds distributed as the will directs, unless all beneficiaries for that gift agree in writing, after the will writer's death, that the gift need not be sold.

If I name two or more primary beneficiaries to receive a specific gift of property and any of them do not survive me, all surviving primary beneficiaries shall equally divide the deceased primary beneficiary's share unless I have specifically provided otherwise. If I name two or more alternate beneficiaries to receive a specific gift of property and any of them do not survive me, all surviving alternate beneficiaries shall equally divide the deceased alternate beneficiary's share.

5. Residuary Estate. I leave my residuary estate, that is, the rest of my property not otherwise specifically and validly disposed of by this will or in any other manner, to

_____ or, if such residuary

beneficiary(ies) do(es) not survive me, to _____

_____

Any residuary gift made in this will to two or more beneficiaries shall be shared equally among them, unless unequal shares are specifically indicated. All shared residuary gifts must be sold, and the net proceeds distributed as the will directs, unless all beneficiaries for that gift agree in writing, after the will writer's death, that the gift need not be sold.

If I name two or more alternate residuary beneficiaries to receive property and any of them do not survive me, all surviving alternate residuary beneficiaries shall equally divide the deceased alternate residuary beneficiary's share.

As used in any section of this will, the word "survive" means to outlive the will writer by at least 45 days.

6. Executor. I name _____
as executor, to serve without bond. If that executor does not qualify, or ceases to serve, I
name _____
as executor, also to serve without bond.

 I direct that my executor take all actions legally permissible to probate this will,
including filing a petition in the appropriate court for the independent administration of my
estate.

 I grant to my executor the following powers, to be exercised as the executor deems to be
in the best interests of my estate:

 (1) To retain property, without liability for loss or depreciation resulting from such
retention.

 (2) To sell, lease or exchange property and to receive or administer the proceeds as a
part of my estate.

 (3) To vote stock, convert bonds, notes, stocks or other securities belonging to my estate
into other securities, and to exercise all other rights and privileges of a person owning similar
property.

 (4) To deal with and settle claims in favor of or against my estate.

 (5) To continue, maintain, operate or participate in any business which is a part of my
estate, and to incorporate, dissolve or otherwise change the form of organization of the
business.

 (6) To pay all debts and taxes that may be assessed against my estate, as provided under
state law.

 (7) To do all other acts, which in the executor's judgment may be necessary or appropriate for the proper and advantageous management, investment and distribution of my estate.

 These powers, authority and discretion are in addition to the powers, authority and
discretion vested in an executor by operation of law, and may be exercised as often as
deemed necessary, without approval by any court in any jurisdiction.

 7. Personal Guardian. If at my death any of my children are minors and a personal
guardian is needed, I name _____
as the personal guardian, to serve without bond. If this person is unable or unwilling to serve
as personal guardian, I name _____
as personal guardian, also to serve without bond.

Form 5

8. Property Guardian. If any of my children are minors and a property guardian is needed, I name _____
as the property guardian, to serve without bond. If this person is unable or unwilling to serve as property guardian, I name _____
as property guardian, also to serve without bond.

9. Children's Trust. All property I leave in this will to any of the beneficiaries listed in Section A, below, shall be held for each of them in a separate trust, administered according to the following terms:

A. Trust Beneficiaries and Age Limits

Each trust shall end when the following beneficiaries become 35 years of age, except as otherwise specified in this section.

Trust Beneficiary	Trust Shall End At Age
_____	_____
_____	_____
_____	_____
_____	_____
_____	_____

B. Trustees

I name _____
as trustee, to serve without bond. If this person is unable or unwilling to serve as trustee, I name _____
as successor trustee, also to serve without bond.

C. Beneficiary Provisions

(1) The trustee may distribute for the benefit of each beneficiary as much of the net income or principal of the trust as the trustee deems necessary for the beneficiary's health, support, maintenance and education. In deciding whether to make a distribution for or to a beneficiary, the trustee may take into account the beneficiary's other income, resources and sources of support.

(2) Any trust income that is not distributed to a beneficiary by the trustee shall be accumulated and added to the principal of the trust administered for that beneficiary.

D. Termination of Trust

The trust shall terminate when any of the following occurs:

(1) The beneficiary becomes the age specified in Paragraph A of this trust;

(2) The beneficiary dies before becoming the age specified in Paragraph A of this trust; or

(3) The trust property is used up through distributions allowed under these provisions.

If the trust terminates because the beneficiary reaches the specified age, the remaining principal and accumulated net income of the trust shall pass to the beneficiary. If the trust terminates because the beneficiary dies, the remaining principal and accumulated net income of the trust shall pass to the trust beneficiary's heirs.

E. Powers of Trustee

In addition to other powers granted to the trustee in this will, the trustee shall have:

(1) All the powers generally conferred on trustees by the laws of the state having jurisdiction over this trust;

(2) With respect to property in the trust, the powers conferred by this will on the executor; and

(3) The authority to hire and pay from the trust assets the reasonable fees of investment advisors, accountants, tax advisors, agents, attorneys and other assistants to administer the trust and manage any trust asset and for any litigation affecting the trust.

F. Trust Administration Provisions

(1) This trust shall be administered independent of court supervision to the maximum extent possible under the laws of the state having jurisdiction over this trust.

(2) The interests of trust beneficiaries shall not be transferable by voluntary or involuntary assignment or by operation of law and shall be free from the claims of creditors and from attachment, execution, bankruptcy or other legal process to the fullest extent permissible by law.

(3) Any trustee serving shall be entitled to reasonable compensation out of the trust assets for ordinary and extraordinary services, and for all services in connection with the complete or partial termination of any trust created by this will.

(4) The invalidity of any provision of this trust instrument shall not affect the validity of the remaining provisions.

I subscribe my name to this will this _____ day of _____, 20___, at _____, State of _____, and declare it is my will, that I sign it willingly, that I execute it as my free and voluntary act for the purposes expressed, and that I am of the age of majority or otherwise legally empowered to make a will and under no constraint or undue influence.

_____
signature

Form 5

Witnesses

On this _____ day of _____, 20___, the testator,
_____, declared to us, the undersigned, that this instrument was his or her will and requested us to act as witnesses to it. The testator signed this will in our presence, all of us being present at the same time. We now, at the testator's request, in the testator's presence, and in the presence of each other, subscribe our names as witnesses and each declare that we are of sound mind and of proper age to witness a will. We further declare that we understand this to be the testator's will, and that to the best of our knowledge the testator is of the age of majority, or is otherwise legally empowered to make a will, and appears to be of sound mind and under no constraint or undue influence.

We declare under penalty of perjury that the foregoing is true and correct, this _____ day of _____, 20___, at _____, State of _____.

_____   _____
        witness's signature   typed or printed name

residing at _____, _____,
             street address   city

_____, _____.
        county   state

_____   _____
        witness's signature   typed or printed name

residing at _____, _____,
             street address   city

_____, _____.
        county   state

_____   _____
        witness's signature   typed or printed name

residing at _____, _____,
             street address   city

_____, _____.
        county   state

Form 5

Beneficiary Property Worksheet

Property Left	Beneficiaries for Specific Gifts	
	Primary Beneficiary(ies)	Alternate Beneficiary(ies)

Additional Specific Gifts

I leave _____

_____

_____

to _____

or, if such beneficiary(ies) do(es) not survive me, to _____

_____

I leave _____

_____

_____

to _____

or, if such beneficiary(ies) do(es) not survive me, to _____

_____

I leave _____

_____

_____

to _____

or, if such beneficiary(ies) do(es) not survive me, to _____

_____

I leave _____

_____

_____

to _____

or, if such beneficiary(ies) do(es) not survive me, to _____

_____

I leave _____

_____

_____

to _____

or, if such beneficiary(ies) do(es) not survive me, to _____

_____

Self-Proving Affidavits

Affidavit-1   *For use by residents of:* Alabama, Alaska, Arizona, Arkansas, Colorado, Connecticut, Hawaii, Idaho, Illinois, Indiana, Maine, Minnesota, Mississippi, Montana, Nebraska, Nevada, New Mexico, New York, North Dakota, Oregon, South Carolina, South Dakota, Tennessee, Utah, Washington and West Virginia.

Affidavit-2   *For use by residents of:* Delaware, Florida, Georgia, Iowa, Kansas, Kentucky, Massachusetts, Missouri, New Jersey, North Carolina, Oklahoma, Pennsylvania, Rhode Island, Virginia and Wyoming.

Affidavit-3   *For use by residents of:* Texas.

Affidavit

We, _____ ,

_____ ,

_____ and

_____ , the

testator and the witnesses, whose names are signed to the attached instrument in those
capacities, personally appearing before the undersigned authority and being first duly sworn,
declare to the undersigned authority under penalty of perjury that:

(1) the testator declared, signed and executed the instrument as his or her last will;

(2) he or she signed it willingly or directed another to sign for him or her;

(3) he or she executed it as his or her free and voluntary act for the purposes therein
expressed; and

(4) each of the witnesses, at the request of the testator, in his or her hearing and
presence, and in the presence of each other, signed the will as witnesses and that to
the best of his or her knowledge the testator was at that time of full legal age, of
sound mind and under no constraint or undue influence.

Testator: _____

Witness: _____
Address: _____

Witness: _____
Address: _____

Witness: _____
Address: _____

Subscribed, sworn and acknowledged before me, _____ ,
a notary public, by _____ ,
the testator, and by _____ ,

_____ ,

and _____ ,
the witnesses, this _____ day of _____ , 20___ .

_____
Signature of notary public

[NOTARY SEAL]   My commission expires: _____

Affidavit 1

Affidavit

STATE OF _____

COUNTY OF _____

    I, the undersigned, an officer authorized to administer oaths, certify that _____

_____, the testator, and

_____,

_____ and

_____, the witnesses,

whose names are signed to the attached or foregoing instrument and whose signatures appear below, having appeared together before me and having been first duly sworn, each then declared to me that:

1) the attached or foregoing instrument is the last will of the testator;
2) the testator willingly and voluntarily declared, signed and executed the will in the presence of the witnesses;
3) the witnesses signed the will upon request by the testator, in the presence and hearing of the testator, and in the presence of each other;
4) to the best knowledge of each witness the testator was, at that time of the signing, of the age of majority (or otherwise legally competent to make a will), of sound mind, and under no constraint or undue influence; and
5) each witness was and is competent, and of the proper age to witness a will.

Testator: _____

Witness: _____

Address: _____

Witness: _____

Address: _____

Witness: _____

Address: _____

Subscribed, sworn and acknowledged before me, _____,

a notary public, by _____,

the testator, and by _____,

_____,

and _____,

the witnesses, this _____ day of _____, 20___.

                     SIGNED: _____

                                  _____

                                  Official Capacity of Officer

Affidavit 2

Affidavit

THE STATE OF TEXAS

COUNTY OF _____

   Before me, the undersigned authority, on this day personally appeared _____

_____, _____

_____, and _____,

known to me to be the testator and the witnesses, respectively, whose names are subscribed

to the annexed or foregoing instrument in their respective capacities, and, all of said persons

being by me duly sworn, the said _____, testator, declared

to me and to the said witnesses in my presence that said instrument is his or her last will

and testament, and that he or she had willingly made and executed it as his or her free act

and deed; and the said witnesses, each on his or her oath stated to me, in the presence and

hearing of the said testator, that the said testator had declared to them that said instrument

is his or her last will and testament, and that he or she executed same as such and wanted

each of them to sign it as a witness; and upon their oaths each witness stated further that

they did sign the same as witnesses in the presence of the said testator and at his or her

request; that he or she was at the time eighteen years of age or over (or being under such

age, was or had been lawfully married, or was then a member of the armed forces of the

United States or an auxiliary thereof or of the Maritime Service) and was of sound mind;

and that each of said witnesses was then at least fourteen years of age.

Testator: _____

Witness: _____

Witness: _____

   Subscribed and sworn to before me by the said _____,

testator, and by the said _____ and

_____ witnesses,

this _____ day of _____,20___.

SIGNED: _____

_____
(Official Capacity of Officer)

Affidavit 3

Will Codicil Form

First Codicil to the Will of _____

I, _____, a resident of _____,
_____, declare this to be the first codicil to my will dated
_____, 20__.

FIRST: I revoke the provision of Section _____, of my will that provided:

and substitute the following :

SECOND: I add the following provision to Section _____:

THIRD: In all other respects I confirm and republish my will dated
_____ , 20__.

Dated _____, 20__.

I subscribe my name to this codicil this _____ day of _____,
20_____, at _____, _____,
        city   county
_____ and do hereby declare, under penalty of perjury,
     state

that I sign and execute this codicil willingly, that I execute it as my free and voluntary act
for the purposes therein expressed, and that I am of the age of majority or otherwise legally
empowered to make a codicil and under no constraint or undue influence.

_____
signature

On this _____ day of _____ , 20___,
_____ declared to us, the undersigned, that this
instrument was the codicil to his/her will and requested us to act as witnesses to it. He/She
thereupon signed this codicil in our presence, all of us being present at the same time. We
now, at his/her request, in his/her presence, and in the presence of each other, subscribe our
names as witnesses and declare we understand this to be his/her codicil and that to the best
of our knowledge he/she is of the age of majority, or is otherwise legally empowered to make
a codicil and is under no constraint or undue influence.

We declare under penalty of perjury that the foregoing is true and correct this _____
day of _____ , 20___ , at _____ .

_____   _____
witness's signature   typed or printed name

residing at _____ , _____ ,
street address   city

_____ , _____ .
county   state

_____   _____
witness's signature   typed or printed name

residing at _____ , _____ ,
street address   city

_____ , _____ .
county   state

_____   _____
witness's signature   typed or printed name

residing at _____ , _____ ,
street address   city

_____ , _____ .
county   state

Index

R

CATALOG

...more from Nolo Press

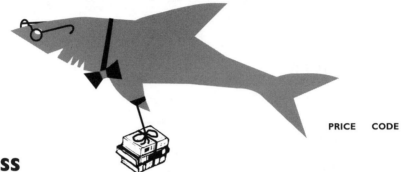

Book with disk
⊙ Book with CD-ROM

	PRICE	CODE
Music Law (Book w/Disk—PC)	$29.95	ML
▣ The Partnership Book: How to Write a Partnership Agreement (Book w/Disk—PC)	$34.95	PART
Sexual Harassment on the Job	$18.95	HARS
Starting and Running a Successful Newsletter or Magazine	$24.95	MAG
Take Charge of Your Workers' Compensation Claim (California Edition)	$29.95	WORK
Tax Savvy for Small Business	$28.95	SAVVY
Trademark: Legal Care for Your Business and Product Name	$29.95	TRD
Wage Slave No More: Law & Taxes for the Self-Employed	$24.95	WAGE
Your Rights in the Workplace	$21.95	YRW

CONSUMER

	PRICE	CODE
Fed Up with the Legal System: What's Wrong & How to Fix It	$9.95	LEG
How to Win Your Personal Injury Claim	$24.95	PICL
Nolo's Everyday Law Book	$21.95	EVL
Nolo's Pocket Guide to California Law	$11.95	CLAW
Trouble-Free Travel...And What to Do When Things Go Wrong	$14.95	TRAV

ESTATE PLANNING & PROBATE

	PRICE	CODE
8 Ways to Avoid Probate (Quick & Legal Series)	$15.95	PRO8
How to Probate an Estate (California Edition)	$34.95	PAE
Make Your Own Living Trust	$24.95	LITR
Nolo's Law Form Kit: Wills	$14.95	KWL
▣ Nolo's Will Book (Book w/Disk—PC)	$29.95	SWIL
Plan Your Estate	$24.95	NEST
The Quick and Legal Will Book (Quick & Legal Series)	$15.95	QUIC

FAMILY MATTERS

	PRICE	CODE
Child Custody: Building Parenting Agreements That Work	$24.95	CUST
Divorce & Money: How to Make the Best Financial Decisions During Divorce	$26.95	DIMO
Do Your Own Divorce in Oregon	$19.95	ODIV
Get a Life: You Don't Need a Million to Retire Well	$18.95	LIFE
The Guardianship Book (California Edition)	$24.95	GB
How to Adopt Your Stepchild in California	$22.95	ADOP
How to Raise or Lower Child Support in California (Quick & Legal Series)	$19.95	CHLD
A Legal Guide for Lesbian and Gay Couples	$24.95	LG
The Living Together Kit	$24.95	LTK
Nolo's Pocket Guide to Family Law	$14.95	FLD

▣ Book with disk

◉ Book with CD-ROM

	PRICE	CODE

GOING TO COURT

	PRICE	CODE
Collect Your Court Judgment (California Edition)	$24.95	JUDG
The Criminal Law Handbook: Know Your Rights, Survive the System	$24.95	KYR
How to Seal Your Juvenile & Criminal Records (California Edition)	$24.95	CRIM
How to Sue For Up to $25,000...and Win!	$29.95	MUNI
Everybody's Guide to Small Claims Court in California	$18.95	CSCC
Everybody's Guide to Small Claims Court (National Edition)	$18.95	NSCC
Fight Your Ticket ... and Win! (California Edition)	$19.95	FYT
How to Change Your Name in California	$29.95	NAME
Mad at Your Lawyer	$21.95	MAD
Represent Yourself in Court: How to Prepare & Try a Winning Case	$29.95	RYC

HOMEOWNERS, LANDLORDS & TENANTS

	PRICE	CODE
The Deeds Book (California Edition)	$16.95	DEED
Dog Law	$14.95	DOG
▣ Every Landlord's Legal Guide (National Edition, Book w/Disk—PC)	$34.95	ELLI
Every Tenant's Legal Guide	$24.95	EVTEN
For Sale by Owner in California	$24.95	FSBO
How to Buy a House in California	$24.95	BHCA
The Landlord's Law Book, Vol. 1: Rights & Responsibilities (California Edition)	$34.95	LBRT
The Landlord's Law Book, Vol. 2: Evictions (California Edition)	$34.95	LBEV
Leases & Rental Agreements (Quick & Legal Series)	$18.95	LEAR
Neighbor Law: Fences, Trees, Boundaries & Noise	$17.95	NEI
Stop Foreclosure Now in California	$29.95	CLOS
Tenants' Rights (California Edition)	$19.95	CTEN

HUMOR

	PRICE	CODE
29 Reasons Not to Go to Law School	$9.95	29R
Poetic Justice	$9.95	PJ

IMMIGRATION

	PRICE	CODE
How to Get a Green Card: Legal Ways to Stay in the U.S.A.	$24.95	GRN
U.S. Immigration Made Easy	$39.95	IMEZ

▣ Book with disk
◉ Book with CD-ROM

		PRICE	CODE

MONEY MATTERS

	PRICE	CODE
▣ 101 Law Forms for Personal Use (Quick and Legal Series, Book w/disk—PC)	$24.95	SPOT
Bankruptcy: Is It the Right Solution to Your Debt Problems? (Quick & Legal Series)	$15.95	BRS
Chapter 13 Bankruptcy: Repay Your Debts	$29.95	CH13
Credit Repair (Quick & Legal Series)	$15.95	CREP
▣ The Financial Power of Attorney Workbook (Book w/disk—PC)	$24.95	FINPOA
How to File for Bankruptcy	$26.95	HFB
IRAs, 401(k)s, & Other Retirement Plans: Taking Your Money Out	$21.95	RET
Money Troubles: Legal Strategies to Cope With Your Debts	$19.95	MT
Nolo's Law Form Kit: Personal Bankruptcy	$16.95	KBNK
Stand Up to the IRS	$24.95	SIRS
Take Control of Your Student Loans	$19.95	SLOAN

PATENTS AND COPYRIGHTS

	PRICE	CODE
▣ The Copyright Handbook: How to Protect and Use Written Works (Book w/disk—PC)	$29.95	COHA
Copyright Your Software	$24.95	CYS
The Inventor's Notebook	$19.95	INOT
▣ License Your Invention (Book w/Disk—PC)	$39.95	LICE
The Patent Drawing Book	$29.95	DRAW
Patent, Copyright & Trademark	$24.95	PCTM
Patent It Yourself	$44.95	PAT
◉ Software Development: A Legal Guide (Book with CD-ROM)	$44.95	SFT

RESEARCH & REFERENCE

	PRICE	CODE
◉ Government on the Net (Book w/CD-ROM—Windows/Macintosh)	$39.95	GONE
◉ Law on the Net (Book w/CD-ROM—Windows/Macintosh)	$39.95	LAWN
Legal Research: How to Find & Understand the Law	$21.95	LRES
Legal Research Made Easy (Video)	$89.95	LRME
◉ Legal Research Online and in the Library (Book w/CD-ROM—Windows/Macintosh)	$39.95	LRO

SENIORS

	PRICE	CODE
Beat the Nursing Home Trap	$18.95	ELD
The Conservatorship Book (California Edition)	$34.95	CNSV
Social Security, Medicare & Pensions	$19.95	SOA

▣ Book with disk

◉ Book with CD-ROM

ORDER FORM

Code	Quantity	Title	Unit price	Total
		Subtotal		
		California residents add Sales Tax		
		Basic Shipping ($6.50)		
		UPS RUSH delivery $8.00–any size order*		
		TOTAL		

Name

Address

(UPS to street address, Priority Mail to P.O. boxes)   * Delivered in 3 business days from receipt of
S.F. Bay Area use regular shipping. order.

FOR FASTER SERVICE, USE YOUR CREDIT CARD & OUR TOLL-FREE NUMBERS

Order 24 hours a day   1-800-992-6656
Fax your order   1-800-645-0895
online   www.nolo.com

METHOD OF PAYMENT

☐ Check enclosed
☐ VISA   ☐ MasterCard   ☐ Discover Card   ☐ American Express

Account #   Expiration Date

Authorizing Signature

Daytime Phone

PRICES SUBJECT TO CHANGE.

VISIT OUR OUTLET   VISIT US ONLINE

You'll find our complete line of books and software, all at a discount.

BERKELEY
950 Parker Street
Berkeley, CA 94710
1-510-704-2248

on the Internet

www.nolo.com

NOLO PRESS 950 PARKER ST., BERKELEY, CA 94710

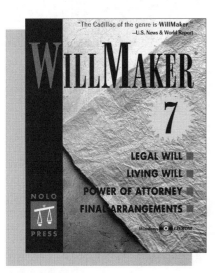
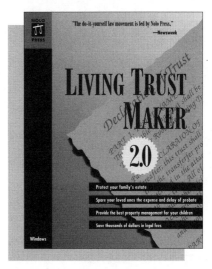

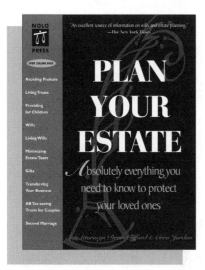
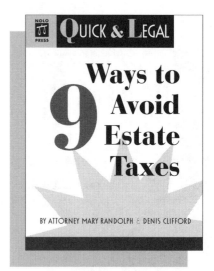

With our quarterly magazine, the **NOLO** *News*, you'll

- **Learn** about important legal changes that affect you
- **Find out first** about new Nolo products
- **Keep current** with practical articles on everyday law
- **Get answers** to your legal questions in *Ask Auntie Nolo's* advice column
- **Save money** with special Subscriber Only discounts
- **Tickle your funny bone** with our famous *Lawyer Joke* column.

It only takes a minute to reserve your free 1-year subscription or to extend your **NOLO** *News* subscription.

CALL	FAX	E-MAIL	**OR MAIL US THIS REGISTRATION CARD**
1-800-992-6656	**1-800-645-0895**	**NOLOSUB@NOLOPRESS.com**	

 *U.S. ADDRESSES ONLY. ONE YEAR INTERNATIONAL SUBSCRIPTIONS: CANADA & MEXICO $10.00; ALL OTHER FOREIGN ADDRESSES $20.00.

fold here

- -

NOLO

PRESS

REGISTRATION CARD

NAME		DATE
ADDRESS		

CITY   STATE   ZIP

PHONE   E-MAIL

WHERE DID YOU HEAR ABOUT THIS PRODUCT?

WHERE DID YOU PURCHASE THIS PRODUCT?

DID YOU CONSULT A LAWYER? (PLEASE CIRCLE ONE)   YES   NO   NOT APPLICABLE

DID YOU FIND THIS BOOK HELPFUL?   (VERY)   5   4   3   2   1   (NOT AT ALL)

COMMENTS

WAS IT EASY TO USE?   (VERY EASY)   5   4   3   2   1   (VERY DIFFICULT)

DO YOU OWN A COMPUTER? IF SO, WHICH FORMAT? (PLEASE CIRCLE ONE)   WINDOWS   DOS   MAC

❑ If you do not wish to receive mailings from these companies, please check this box.

❑ You can quote me in future Nolo Press promotional materials. Daytime phone number _____.   QUIC 2.0

NOLO IN THE NEWS

"**N**olo helps lay people perform legal tasks without the aid—or fees—of lawyers."

—**USA TODAY**

Nolo books are ..."written in plain language, free of legal mumbo jumbo, and spiced with witty personal observations."

—**ASSOCIATED PRESS**

"...Nolo publications...guide people simply through the how, when, where and why of law."

—**WASHINGTON POST**

"Increasingly, people who are not lawyers are performing tasks usually regarded as legal work... And consumers, using books like Nolo's, do routine legal work themselves."

—**NEW YORK TIMES**

"...All of [Nolo's] books are easy-to-understand, are updated regularly, provide pull-out forms...and are often quite moving in their sense of compassion for the struggles of the lay reader."

—**SAN FRANCISCO CHRONICLE**

fold here

- -

Place
stamp here

NOLO
PRESS

NOLO PRESS
950 Parker Street
Berkeley, CA 94710-9867

Attn: | **QUIC 2.0**